Home Sweet Home

homespun stories from the sunny side of life

Kristen Howard

© 2021 C&S Christian Publishing

All rights reserved. No part of this publication may be reproduced, distributed, or transmitted in any form in by any means, including photocopying, recording, or other electronic mechanical methods, without, the prior written permission of the publisher, except in the case of brief quotations embodied in critical reviews and certain other noncommercial uses permitted by copyright law. This book was printed in the United States of America.

All Scripture quotations, unless otherwise indicated, are taken from the Holy Bible, New International Version®. NIV®. Copyright © 1973, 1978, 1984 by International Bible Society.

Scripture quotations marked KJV are from the Holy Bible, King James Version (Authorized Version). First published in 1611. Quoted from the KJV Classic Reference Bible, Copyright 1983 by The Zondervan Corporation.

Scriptures marked NLT are taken from the HOLY BIBLE, NEW LIVING TRANSLATION (NLT): Scriptures taken from the HOLY BIBLE, NEW LIVING TRANSLATION, Copyright© 1996, 2004, 2007 by Tyndale House Foundation. Used by permission of Tyndale House Publishers, Inc., Carol Stream, Illinois 60188. All rights reserved. Used by permission.

Scriptures marked AMP are taken from the AMPLIFIED BIBLE (AMP): Scripture taken from the AMPLIFIED® BIBLE, Copyright © 1954, 1958, 1962, 1964, 1965, 1987 by the Lockman Foundation Used by Permission. (www.Lockman.org

Acknowledgements

This book is dedicated to my family. The stories collected along life's way have created a beautiful backdrop in which to share God's faithfulness and love for His heartbeat - the family and the home.

Chuck and Eva, thank you for making me a better wife and mother each day. It is in my mistakes that I find value and try again. You both are my world. Life doesn't seem right if we are not together. Chuck, thank you for pushing me past frustration and teaching me to win. As you have told me often, *"Life doesn't pass out participation awards."* Eva, thank you for seeing the sunny side of life. I love being your mommy and cherish our time together. Watching you grow is the best reward a mother could earn. You are counting on me. I won't let you down.

To my Mother and Father, no one could see the stories as they were being lived but what a collection they created. Mom, thank you for teaching me to be a lady, to stand tall, and to carry a purse. My life is a direct reflection of your sacrifice. You chose to be a mother first. I am forever grateful. Pops, thank you for all the life lessons woven into everyday life. Thank you for teaching me discipline and for telling me about the view from the top. It keeps me climbing.

To my sister Brittney, I have heard it said, *"A sister is growing up with your best friend."* Thank you for all your winks, stares, throat clears and all your jokes, but most importantly, thank you for your friendship. Life is so much better with you in it!

Contents

Are You Just a Bricklayer? 1
Mary Poppins 4
Picture Perfect 8
Alan Jackson 11
Looking for Mayberry 14
Broken Eggs 18
The Kitchen Table 21
The Grinch 25
It's a Wonderful Life 29
Letters to Santa 33
The Spirit of Christmas Past 37
And Forget Not All His Benefits 40
You Will Never Make General 44
Eye of the Tiger 47
I Have an Appointment 51
For Sale: One Used Saddle 56
Date Night 60
I DO 64
There's a Giant Inside 69
A Picture of Happy 73
The Ride 76
Good Night, Sweet Dreams, I Love You, I Will See You In The Morning 80
Making Offers On Memories 85
The Finish Line 88
Like Arrows 92

Waving Palm Branches 97
Living on Borrowed Time 102
Gather Round for Prayer 105
April 27th, 2011 109
A Place to Call Home 115
It'll Wash 120
Pen Pals 123
Getting My Hands Dirty 127
Life is Just Better in the Country 131
Swimming Lessons 135
The Grill 139
Sugar and Spice and Everything Nice 143
The Fourth of July Parade 148
In a Pasture Somewhere 153
All for a Cinnamon Roll 158
Mother's Biscuits 163
Because I Said So 168
More Days Like Today 172
Oh Be Careful Little Eyes What You See 176
Kinks in the Electrical Cord 180
Bosom Friends 184
Remember Who You Are 189
Happy Camper 194
Cheese and Crackers 199
A Handful of Dandelions 203
Living Waters Fellowship 206
Paint the Dragons Red 211
Twenty Winks 215

"You are the gatekeeper into your home." This statement echoes in my ears before many of life's daily practical needs take place. What comes into my home and what my children are exposed to outside of these four walls is up to my husband and I to guard. No one will do it like Mommy and Daddy. As you read through these short stories of my everyday life, both past and present, you too will find it amazing how God shows up on the scene unannounced with quiet whispers of the way we should follow.

"Righteousness goes before Him and prepares the way for His steps." Psalms 85:13

ARE YOU JUST A BRICKLAYER?

As we sat in church listening to our pastor, He made a statement that went deep inside my heart. He said, *"Are you just a Bricklayer or do you know what you're building?"* I found myself at the altar that morning knowing, I would leave changed. Repentance, by definition means, to turn or make a change and that is exactly what was happening to me.

I had a new destination I desired for my family, and I knew we would not drift there. It would require us to set our course. It was going to be hard work, and demand a backstage pass into my home. It was not time for applause or a standing ovation. It was time to pick up the shovel and get to work.

I decided I was not going to just lay bricks without a blueprint for what I was building. Whether it's wiping a runny nose, cleaning up juice spills, folding laundry, cooking, scrubbing toilets or reading bedtime stories, I had found my purpose.

I am the heart of my home, and my family is counting on me. This is every wife and mother's highest calling. It is my job to pour in purpose, destiny, future and hope. The tasks are not meaningless but resolute. I am building the next generation. The most important ministry I will ever have happens between the four walls of my home.

God has put inside each wife and mother the abilities we need to make our homes a haven, a safe place. A place where our families come and find peace, solitude, and comfort. Brick by brick, we watch them grow and teach them by example how to repent and forgive. Home is where the Word of God should be lived the loudest.

The family unit is the building block upon which a society is built. A strong family, a Biblically-minded family, will become a society that is thriving and will create a culture that refuses to bend to a world pulling in the opposite direction.

There are some basic fundamental truths that we as families must get back to. We must guard our homes against life's many intruders. We are the gatekeeper of our homes. This can only be done by the principles outlined in God's Word, which are practical freeing truths that, when applied to our everyday life, bring structure and purpose. Faith and family are at the very core of who God is. He deeply desires to show us his heart. It starts in the home.

I hope you will join me as we set our course back to the basics and perhaps ask yourself the same question I was asked: *Are you just a bricklayer or do you know what you are building?*

Welcome Home

A wise woman builds her home, but a foolish woman tears it down with her own hands. Proverbs 14:1

MARY POPPINS

It was practically perfect in every way. The invitations were, of course, *"Theme printed"* and specialty ordered. I had a toy room scene set up as you walked in our front door, and you could hear the Disney soundtrack to *Mary Poppins* playing in the background; homemade kites were hanging from the ceiling, toy blocks spelling out *Mary Poppins* were positioned just right. Obviously, carnations were everywhere. *"Feed the bird"* bags were placed outside with tuppence (two-pence) surrounding.

There was a serving table draped with a beautiful red tablecloth. It had an old tailor's tape running down the center. Gracing the table were; *Chimney Sweeps* for Bert, *Spoonsful of Sugar* for Mary Poppins, and *Caramel Apple Bites* for Jane and Michael. Not to mention the macaroni and cheese, grilled chicken and homemade dips; all served on fine matching platters and labeled accordingly. For a beverage, I served Raspberry punch, taken from the medicinal scene, where Mary Poppins has the children take their medicine.

No party is complete without the cake! And this cake truly was *Supercalifragilisticexpialidocious*! It was a two-tiered round cake with the most elaborate and unique *Mary Poppins* designs. Outside I had the tables covered with cream tablecloths. Charcoal and carnations were arranged as the centerpiece and a joke card was placed at each seat from Uncle Albert's laughing scene.

Everything was color coordinated, from the balloons to *Bert's sidewalk magic* (party favor). I even had *Mary Poppins* t-shirts made for Eva and me so we would match in our outfits. What a party this was going to be! As I was tacking up the last kite, my husband asked me why I was doing all this? I told him it was because I wanted Eva to have the best. He just nodded and walked off. I should have pressed him for his input, but I brushed it off and continued on with my own agenda.

When my folks arrived and saw all that I had done, I put my arm around my dad and said, *"Isn't this just great?" "I did all this for Eva."* He just looked at me, and unlike Chuck, he holds nothing back. He said, *"NO, you didn't do all this for Eva." "You did all of this for you,"* I said nothing.

The birthday came off without a hitch, and everyone had a

great time. But my thoughts were on my dad's comment. He was right, and I knew it. Eva didn't care that everything was color coordinated or that the party games were Mary Poppins inspired. She was two years old. All she cared about was cake and throwing wrapping paper everywhere.

I was too caught up in appearance and needed to make some changes. I decided when her next birthday came around it would genuinely be about her.

A year passed in a flash. My first order of business was to purchase handwritten invitations. My second assignment was to make sure the guest list did not exceed her five favorite friends. When it was time for party supplies, I loaded her up in the car and took her to our favorite store. We headed straight for the plastic party aisle. Once there, I took her out of the cart and told her I needed her help picking out all her party supplies. Her eyes beamed with excitement! She went down that aisle grabbing plates, cups, napkins, forks, spoons, tablecloths, streamers, hats, and bubbles. Nothing matched, and I loved it. No theme. Just good old-fashioned birthday party fun.

As we made her birthday cake that night (a Duncan Hines special) and I watched her eat spoonsful of batter, while we laughed and played, something changed in me. I saw what was truly important.

I thought I was doing Eva a favor by throwing her an

elaborate birthday party, but in reality, I was crippling her. I was setting a standard I could not begin to live up to. Offering a taste of life that does not exist, a figment of her imagination that was intended to create an imaginary wonderland would in return create a monster; a monster I would not be able to harness.

Birthday parties are wonderful, and it is easy to get them out of proportion; personally, relationally, and financially. I want to run my race like a champion, and I cannot do that trying to keep up with Mr. and Mrs. Jones'.

As Eva grows, her Birthday parties may change, but for this one, I found valuable lessons learned for my own personal benefit. It's funny. Mary Poppins taught me more as an adult than she ever did as a child.

Welcome Home

Let us lay aside every weight and sin which so easily ensnares us and let us run with endurance the race that is set before us. Hebrews 12:1

Picture Perfect

Each year around October, we have our family photos taken. My mother did this as I grew up and now, I carry on the tradition for my family. I always enjoy seeing how much my family changes each year.

As I hung our recent family portrait on the wall, a thought occurred to me, "*We look absolutely perfect.*" Every hair was in place, our outfits coordinated exceptionally well; everyone was smiling, holding hands, and loving each other. Even the dogs sat faultlessly as if posing for Purina dog chow. Our family looked flawless.

Oh, but if pictures could talk, what a story they would tell! The before and after look nothing like the portrait that graces our wall. By the time the photo session is over, the dogs are running wild, Eva is sobbing, and Chuck has already removed his new Polo and is now sporting his favorite t-shirt.

We portray in a snapshot what real life looks nothing like. Those smiling faces hanging on the wall tell nothing of the long days and short attitudes. The perfectly positioned print shows no indication of the over-grown yard in dire need of lawn care or the supper left burning on the stove while you frantically chase down a naked toddler, who is now peeing in the backyard. No one sees the play-dough that lies smashed on the kitchen table waiting for you to scrape it clean, or the little handprints left all over the walls. Sweat, dirt and grime seem to be the style for young mothers and showers are a thing of the past. Hidden in looks and glances, there is an apology owed to your spouse, but through the busyness, it ends up sent by text message to the wrong person. These are the real moments that are never captured in the frame.

I like to tell people, *"We are a family under construction but building on the right foundation."* It is in seeing the errors and making necessary changes that bring improvement; learning to work together to navigate life's many challenges.

Last year, for our anniversary, Chuck and I spent a quiet evening at home enjoying his famous spaghetti. Our love story is a lot like *Lady and the Tramp*. I fell in love with him over a bowl full of spaghetti, and he still knows it is the way to my heart.

Once supper was finished, we found ourselves sitting on the

Home Sweet Home

back porch looking through our family albums. Flipping through the pictures, we found the years were showing us things the days never did. We saw laughter and tears, trials and triumphs. It was a story that, at the time, had been unwritten.

Life takes a little longer to develop than one snapshot. I heard it said somewhere, *"A Christian with the greatest life is a Christian with the greatest memories."*

Hang your pictures and enjoy the imperfections. God will fine-tune, as you continue together and what a beautiful picture He will create.

Welcome Home

"Be kind and affectionate toward one another with brotherly love, in honor, giving preference to one another." Romans 12:3

ALAN JACKSON

Country music is one of my all-time favorite music genres. I grew up in cowboy country, so it is only natural that I would love it. My favorite songs are the ones about faith, family and the simple life.

By no means am I a concert groupie, but on occasion, I like to go see the older country music artists. Alan Jackson is one of those legends.

Several years ago, I received a phone call from a friend of mine. She had two Alan Jackson tickets to give away and wanted to know if I would like them. I immediately gave a resounding, *"YES!"* I knew my husband would be coming home that same day from a two-week work trip overseas and would not be interested in going, but I also knew he would tell me to go

Home Sweet Home

because he knew how much I enjoyed Alan Jackson.

Without any hesitation, I quickly called another friend of mine and offered her the other ticket. She was excited and agreed to go. Next, I called and got our babysitter lined up for that night. Everything was arranged beautifully, and I was thrilled!

I decided to call and tell my mom about the concert, knowing she would be excited for me. Dad was around, listening to me tell Mom my news. As I finished, I heard nothing but silence on the other end. It was the kind of silence where I instantly knew I had messed up royally.

With my parents, especially my dad, they have a very gentle yet firm way of correcting. I heard my dad softly say, *"You are willing to let your husband come home after a two-week work trip and find his house empty, while you are off at an Alan Jackson concert?"* If that wasn't enough, he continued on. *"Further, you are willing to go with your friend when he would much prefer to be the one going with you?"*

My heart sank. I hadn't realized the unspoken message it would send to my husband when he came home and found me gone. He never would have uttered a word about it, but deep down, he would have thought, as any man would, *"I work and provide, and she isn't even here to greet me?"*

Needless to say, I canceled my plans, and when my husband walked in the door, he found our little girl and me waiting for him. We had front row seats because the real star was walking on the stage. Eva and I had our BIG hugs waiting for him. With tears in my eyes, I shared my heart with him. Can I tell you, he stood a little taller that day.

Ladies, our actions are powerful. The home is your sanctuary. It's a place where your husband should find you present. Our absence should be a rare occasion. But our presence should be a sweet aroma and fragrance every time he walks through that door. Everything might not be perfect, but the fact that we are home builds him up and shows him we honor and appreciate him.

I don't want to be found guilty of making so many plans of my own that I forget the value of being home. Alan Jackson can wait, but my husband cannot.

Welcome Home

"The heart of her husband safely trusts her….She does him good and not evil all the days of her life." Proverbs 31:11,12

LOOKING FOR MAYBERRY

"The Andy Griffith Show" is my all-time favorite show. Every day at lunch-time, my folks would watch it, and now, a day doesn't go by that an *Andy Griffith* line doesn't fit somewhere. For example, when the weather is not to your liking, you can say, *"Everyone complains about the weather, but nobody does anything about it."* Or when something must be done immediately and thoroughly, you can say, *"Fast, clean."* Then there's my favorite. If something goes wrong, you can say, *"Call the man!"*

The entertainment was clean and wholesome. It was a show that found humor in the ordinary day in and day out of life. The town of Mayberry depicted a simpler time; predictable and stable; a forgotten way perhaps. It was a place where everything was black and white.

Perhaps a little bigger than Mayberry, but the town I grew up in had the same hometown feel. People knew their neighbors and the latest stories from the morning paper. There was a local hardware store, grocery store, and barbershop. It was a place where a leisurely bike ride through town would always end with a sweet treat from the timeless classic of, *Zesto*.

Pierre, South Dakota, is located in the heart of cowboy country, so it is only natural that we would have an annual Fourth of July parade and rodeo. Our parade came with a horse and rider section, which held flags from all fifty states and a rodeo that never disappointed with its saddle bronc and bull riding!

It was a town where children still walked to school, field trips were common-place and cupcakes were a standard birthday treat. Sunday mornings always drew a crowd, and for our church, this was no exception. Most stores were closed on Sundays, and people enjoyed time with their families. December brought snow, crackling fireplaces, and Christmas trees that lined the Capital building. A dear old family friend of ours used to say, *"Home is where you raise your kids."* He couldn't have been more right. Pierre will always be my childhood home.

No longer living in a small town but in a larger city, I find myself, *"Lookin' for Mayberry."* Wondering silently, where it all went? A small-town girl with small-town ways could get lost in a big city like this one, if I wasn't intentional, that is.

At first, I tried to keep up with all the ripping and running, but I quickly realized that wasn't for me or my family. I was reminded of my growing up years and how my parents intentionally made sure life stayed slow and easy. They set limits on our extracurricular activities and how much time we spent away from home. There were chores to be done and homework to be checked. We had a set supper time, family time and bedtime. The days were not complicated. They were ordinary.

In a fast-paced society, success moves slowly. It is not what we do once that brings results. It is what we do over and over again. Success will require a constant effort to maintain a life of stability with values that are black and white.

Mayberry is not just a fictional town. It's a way of life. It's an atmosphere you create and restrictions you set.

Life has a way of suffocating the simple and crowding out the important things. Chuck and I have learned to take notice when we see this pattern developing and stop it before it gets out of control. Our priorities become rechecked, and limits are reset. We are determined to live our lives at home, together, with a Mayberry feel. We cannot expect a strong home if our foundation is constantly moving.

The fast and furious comes to everyone, but that should be the exception, not the rule. I heard it put best, *"Some people seek beautiful places while others make places beautiful."* I don't want to spend my life, "*Lookin for Mayberry.*" I want to create it, right where I am.

Welcome Home

"My people will live in safety, quietly at home and they will be at rest."
Isaiah 32:18

BROKEN EGGS

Broken eggs laid all over the kitchen floor. Yellow egg yolks were dripping down the counter-tops as if keeping tempo with my frantic thoughts. I saw an empty egg carton lying on the kitchen floor, and next to it stood a little girl about three feet tall. She had curly brown hair and big brown eyes. In her hand, she held the only remaining egg. As she handed, what seemed to be a golden egg out to me, she said, *"I tried to get this for you, Mommy."*

    Tired and my head a little fuzzy from all the morning activities, I was in much need of some peace and quiet while Eva took her afternoon nap. Instead, as I hauled in the last couple of bags of groceries, I was met with disaster. Weary can be a dangerous place to meet disaster. That is usually the place where we say things we don't mean, discipline wrong, or speak too harshly.

All those things crossed my mind, but instead, I took a deep breath and closed my eyes. It was at that moment I heard the words, *"Love mercy."* I saw my mother in a flash, and I smiled, knowing exactly what I would do.

I bent down ever so gently and said, *"Eva, it's ok. We don't punish for accidents."* I hugged her and told her we had a BIG mess to clean up! She laughed and ran to grab her little mop.

Disciplining at the wrong time would not get the results I desired, correction and patience would. This was an opportunity to teach a valuable lesson. Accidents do not magically go away. Showing her the process of cleaning up and teaching her the importance of waiting for Mommy before climbing the counter to grab an egg will do more for her in the long run than misguided anger in the name of discipline. Discipline comes into play after the teaching has been ignored.

As parents, we sometimes forget this crucial step. I, too, have had my moments of regret but have learned from them. I had the privilege of growing up in a home where this principle was taught by example so well. I can remember many times receiving mercy when I should have received a punishment.

Oh, there were many times I received the board of correction across the seat of knowledge, and I know, all too well, the sound leather makes as it comes through the belt loops, but I have also seen a father who would walk away before correcting his children, simply because he knew he was too mad to handle it at that moment.

I have seen my father not once, but every time before a spanking, make sure that I knew how much he loved me. Because of their example and astute guidance, I knew the course I needed to take at this moment.

There is a fine line between mercy, judgement, and instruction. It's only in the application of God's word that we find that balance. As a parent, there will be plenty of occasions that require a firm hand, but this was not one of them. This was simply broken eggs.

Welcome Home

"Seek justice, love mercy, walk humbly with your God." Micah 6:8

The Kitchen Table

Growing up, there were two things my mother was famous for, hospitality and sweet tea. Therefore, with Thanksgiving around the corner, I cannot think of a more fitting topic to share than a story about my mother's kitchen table.

She believed there was always room for one more, especially at Thanksgiving. I have seen my mother lay a piece of plyboard over two sawhorses, cover it with a tablecloth and connect it to our kitchen table. It would stretch from one end of the house to the other, but everyone would be together, and for her, that was the only way to celebrate Thanksgiving.

It wasn't anything fancy, just a standard dining room table that seated four, six if the center leaf was added. What I wouldn't give to have that table now? I can still see the kitchen towel resting on her shoulder. My mother was never without it, using it to wipe her hands instead of an apron. The reminiscent smells in the kitchen as she cooked are never far away. If I listen carefully, I can hear her holler down the hallway for us girls to come set the table and put ice in the glasses. My mother wasn't a cookbook star, but neither was she willing to give *"take out"* the star award.

I cannot remember every meal served or every conversation we had, but their faces and their laughter are imprinted on my heart forever. Our kitchen table was never cluttered with household bills, piles of laundry or the day's dirty dishes. It was always prepared for its purpose, the gathering. Supper was at five-thirty, and no one was ever late for meals in our house. This was a time for eating and talking, laughing and sharing about the day. Yes, even correction occurred at our supper table, but it was never a place for fighting or bickering. Every meal began with prayer, then dishes were passed, and the meal commenced. The phone was not answered during mealtimes. It could wait. We were valuable. Our kitchen table was precious.

I heard my father say once, *"There are a lot of things said around a kitchen table, leave them there."*

Plastic was not used in our home unless it was an extremely rare occasion, like an outdoor birthday party or dying Easter eggs. The plastic industry thinks they are doing us a favor by giving us more quality time with easy clean-up, but the truth is, plastic robs us of family time and interaction.

Work builds relationship; setting the table, washing dishes, peeling potatoes and stirring the beans. The memories of heart to heart talks while clearing the table or drying a dish are endless for me. I cannot even begin to count how many lessons I have learned just by a broken glass. It's because of a broken glass that I knew how to handle a broken egg. No amount of plasticware can give me those kinds of quality moments. Because of my mother, there is not a large plastic section in my kitchen, nor do I offer guests in my home a plastic bottle of water, but a glass of water. It spells hospitality. It spells home.

This Thanksgiving, I am thankful for the Godly example the Lord placed before me in my mother. What a legacy to pass down; not to mention the recipes, and her biscuits, cornbread, and pecan pie are incomparable.

Ordering pizza is fun, and we enjoy it, but it is a treat, not a staple. Eating out is equally enjoyable, but it will not produce in our families what the kitchen table will.

There is an interesting fact about Olive trees. They spend seven to ten years developing and maturing into their fruitfulness. By age ten, in our own children, the groundwork has already been established. Leave a foundation worth building on, so as they continue to grow, they will want to meet you around the kitchen table.

Home Sweet Home

Welcome Home

"Your wife will be like a fruitful vine within your house. Your children will be like olive trees all around your table." Psalms 128:3

The Grinch

"…The Grinch hated Christmas; The whole Christmas season! Now please don't ask why, no one quite knows the reason. It could be perhaps, that his shoes were too tight. It could be his head wasn't screwed on just right; But I think that the most likely reason of all, may have been that his heart was two sizes too small…" Dr. Seuss

Most of us know someone who acts just like the Grinch as the Christmas season commences. They complain about the decorations, the shopping, the traffic and the pounds of fruit cake delivered to their door. Their Christmas tree lies disassembled in the attic, next to the knotted twinkle lights that burned out years ago.

A Grinch sees Christmas traditions as a thing of the past without any present value. Commercialism has stolen from them the very heart of Christmas and has left them with a cynical viewpoint.

For the Howard's, nothing could be further from the truth. I will admit I probably go overboard, but for me, it is the most wonderful time of year! As I open the storage boxes one by one, memories spring to life once again: Christmas beads, garland and bulbs, snow globes, figurines, and stockings. Baking tins are full of sugary treats, forcing peppermint and spice to linger in the air.

The nostalgic scent of pine fills the room as Christmas trees are adorned with family memories. Beautiful packages, tied up in bows, lie underneath the tree with everyone waiting in anticipation for what's inside. Christmas cards parade up the wall, and Bing Crosby sings in the background while families enjoy all the holiday cheer.

I love to see Christmas wreaths complimenting front doors and homes twinkling like gigantic gingerbread houses. A spirit of giving sweeps over every heart. Smiles embellish children's faces as cookies and milk are set out for Santa Claus, who will undoubtedly be coming down the chimney to leave all of his Christmas wishes under the tree.

In all of it's magic, the true meaning of Christmas comes to life in our home as we set out the Nativity scene. Eva loves to hear me tell the story of baby Jesus asleep in the manger. Sharing the story with her makes me wonder what it might have been like on that first Christmas night?

Is it barely possible that even in Mary's immovable faith and unquestionable obedience that she found herself questioning, *"How could the King of Kings be born in an old stable that smelled of barn animals and moldy hay?"*

What thoughts must have been racing through Joseph's mind? By law, He had the right to walk away, even to have Mary stoned, but he didn't. What kind of mercy does that? Joseph trusted in a God he could not see and in a Word that he could not ignore. He chose to be a father to a son that was not his by birth but his by choice.

As I place the wise men around the manger, a thought occurred to me. They knew the constellations and the meaning behind this star. These wise men had read the scrolls. They knew the prophecies of old. They knew if they followed the star, it would bring them face to face with their savior. Wise men are still laying their gifts at the master's feet.

Could God have planned it this way? That the Great Shepherd was born in a stable, in order for lowly shepherds, who watched over their flocks by night, to know He had come to save them too. I can hear the stable animals talking one to another, saying, *"How wondrous that He would choose to be born right here with all of us, and we would get to spend a little time with Him."* Before he was the Great Shepherd, he was the sacrificial lamb. It's no wonder the

Lamb of God was born in a barn.

The final piece unwrapped is the Angel, I share with Eva about a host of heavenly angels that sing, *"Glory to God in the highest, peace on earth and goodwill toward men!"*

The true meaning of Christmas is entwined in all of our wonderful traditions. It is about a Savior that came to light our way and to give us the gift of eternal life, a gift that is available to all who would simply receive it. It's only when our perception changes that our attitude change also.

Don't tuck Christmas away in the attic and deem it of no value. It's a special time with a rich heritage. Set up your tree, hang your stockings, string your lights, and perhaps, you too will discover what the Grinch uncovered…

"…He puzzled and puzzled till his puzzler was sore. Then the Grinch thought of something he hadn't before. Maybe Christmas, he thought…doesn't come from a store. Maybe Christmas, perhaps…means a little bit more!" Dr. Seuss

Welcome Home

"For unto us a child is born, unto us a son is given: and the government shall be upon his shoulders and His name shall be called Wonderful, Counselor, Mighty God, Everlasting Father, Prince of Peace." Isaiah 9:6-7

It's a Wonderful Life

George Bailey wanted out of Bedford Falls more than anyone ever did. Yet, for one reason or another, he was always passed over. The Building and Loan had him trapped. He knew he had to stay, for they would vote with Potter otherwise. George couldn't see the home he was building for all the improvements it needed. He couldn't see a wife that loved him or children that praised him. All George could see were shattered dreams and a dead-end town. George Bailey was continually looking to the end of his story instead of enjoying the page he was on.

We recently sold our house and moved into our camper while we are transitioning to our dream home in the country. For us, there are not many things we enjoy more than the beautiful countryside, an open fire pit and a charcoal grill smoking. You can believe me when I say this because my husband buys charcoal by the truckload and stacks it in our garage. We grill so much it is cheaper for us to buy in bulk!

However, it is easy to start questioning God's plan when the shower and toilet are basically the same unit. Normal conversation should never involve asking your husband if the tanks have been released. One morning, this very thing happened. As Chuck went out to handle the tanks, I sarcastically asked him to gather the eggs on his way back in. Learning to laugh along the way makes the journey worthwhile.

The day we moved out of our house and set up camp, I saw a side of my husband that I seemed to have missed. He has the patience of Job. It was raining sideways, and yet, Chuck never uttered a word. He simply put on his rain gear and handled one job after the next, soaking wet. I am now on a first-name basis with the folks down at the laundry mat. I haven't decided if this is a good thing or a bad thing? Based on their looks when I drive up, it is questionable.

Camping has provided us with many obstacles to overcome. There is nothing on this camper that my husband has not fixed or repaired in the short time we have been here. Yet, no matter the circumstance, Chuck has never been jostled or jolted into making hasty decisions. He is calculated and steady.

I, on the other hand, can be a lot like George Bailey, in a hurry to get to the end of the book and see how it turns out. I can see God's humor in all of this as I am walking back and forth from the bathhouse with a toddler. I just kind of look up and offer him a bit of a sideways wink and keep going.

Unlike Chuck, I tend to get frustrated when my dreams do not look like the picture I have etched in my mind. Perhaps, if I am not careful, I will miss the beautiful painting found on the canvas. Each page of the story has a purpose. By jumping to the end, we will never see how the story unfolded. I do not want to get to the end of my life and realize I rushed through all the uncomfortable parts. What a tragedy to miss out on a tiny Christmas tree decorated with homemade ornaments or a single strand of lights that twinkled through the window. I hope I never forget how it feels to crowd around a one-sided table and watch tiny hands, covered in frosting, assemble a gingerbread house. When this is all over, I will cherish my husband's gentle hugs and the whispers that everything will be ok.

A thirty-one-foot camper will test the limits of anyone, and yet Eva is convinced she is living the dream. I think she may be right. She has chosen to live the dream while I am still searching for it. Dreams are not found; they are lived. George Bailey found this to be true. A house doesn't make a home, the people inside do.

Our Pastor recently said, *"We live by promises, not explanations."* Trusting the Lord's plan is not always easy but necessary. I know I will find the blessing of the Lord along the pathway of my obedience.

At the end of the movie, *It's a Wonderful Life*, Harry Bailey makes a toast to his brother, George Bailey, and says, *"A toast, to my big brother, George, the richest man in town."* I am not sure what you are facing this Christmas season, but I pray you will enjoy all the riches life has to offer. It truly is a wonderful life.

Welcome Home

"…I have learned the secret to being content in any and every situation, whether well fed or hungry, whether living in plenty or in want. I can do all things through Christ who gives me strength." Philippians 4:12-13

LETTERS TO SANTA

When my sister and I were little girls, we would sit down with the JC Penny Catalog and circle all of the toys we wanted for Christmas. After we knew what we wanted, we would take out our pen and paper and begin to write our letters to Santa. Once we were finished, we would give it to mommy and daddy, believing it would make its way safely into Santa's hands.

Children understand that seeing is not believing, believing is seeing. However, something happens as we grow up. We come to the knowledge that Santa Claus is not real. We learn letters to Santa do not make dreams come true. So, as adults, we tuck our pen and paper away and quit dreaming.

We were living in Pierre, South Dakota, on Grant Street, in a two-story duplex apartment. My parents were a young married

Home Sweet Home

couple with two small children. They had recently just started a church called Living Waters Fellowship. As a kid, my sister and I did not know the difference between an apartment or a house. All that mattered to us was sliding down the stairs in our pajamas as fast as I could!

However, my parents knew the difference. They dreamed of owning their own home in the country. Back then, both my parents were learning to walk by faith and to believe God for the impossible. My dad is a very practical man, and my mother is a dreamer. One day, they were out riding the back roads, just taking some time away to enjoy the countryside. Now, back roads in the Midwest are all dirt roads. I encourage you, if you have never gone down an old dirt road, find one. It will teach you more than blacktop ever could.

As my folks were driving along, they saw twenty acres of land for sale — the most beautiful piece of property they had ever seen. There was a flowing creek with big cottonwood trees and rolling hills in the background. You could watch the sun rise over the hills as it spotlighted a sea of grass, or you could catch a harvest moon creep over the sky at dusk and hear the coyotes howling in unison, looking for a warm place to bed down.

My mother was captivated. She immediately told my dad they would build a house on that land. My father looked at her and said, *"Babe. That's just a pipe dream."* My mother never missed a beat. She replied, *"Yes, but I believe in pipe dreams."*

We spent ten wonderful years on that pipe dream property, 953 Dry Run Road. My father and grandpa constructed the house my mother dreamed about. My sister and I hammered down the floor that became the family room, bedrooms, and kitchen. We stained every piece of baseboard that would run along the base of each wall. My mother painted every room. We watched a house become a home, a house that built me.

My father built twenty acres of fence, with my mother beside him, step for step. He taught us girls how to scrape and set cedar posts to last a lifetime. We learned what hard work was all about; relationships, character and sweat. My mother had her chicken coup out back and would cook fresh eggs almost every morning, and many evenings, chicken was on the menu (pause for hat removal). More cups of sugar were borrowed and returned on that dirt road than I can count. If I got up early enough in the mornings, I could catch my dad staring out the window with a cup of coffee in his hand, watching deer trek through the snow in the backyard as the frost lay heavy on the trees.

There is nothing like being bundled up tight listening to the sound of horse's hooves crunching through the snow as you are being pulled on a horse-drawn bobsled, and off in the distance seeing smoke coming up from the chimney; knowing inside awaits you a cup of hot chocolate by the fire. If only time allowed me to recall all of the sledding adventures and ice-skating on the neighbor's pond. It sounds like a dream, but it was real. I have memories on Dry Run Road that I wouldn't trade for all the gold in China; friendships for a lifetime.

As we see our dreams laid out before us, we begin to believe it. It is the same concept as the house plan my grandpa drew up. When my parents saw the blueprint of their house, something came alive on the inside; it's spiritual. God designed us that way.

The Bible is full of profound truths that, when applied in our life, will change our circumstances. Faith is not a formula for just getting things, and it is certainly not Santa Claus. Faith is an applied principle to every area of our lives. Faith is the key that releases the windows of heaven into our situation, yes, even our dreams. Sitting around, hoping dreams will come true, will not do any good. Hope only keeps me smiling, but faith will cause me to seize the promise!

God never intended for us to grow up and quit dreaming; look around. God is a dreamer himself. He is very clear about his words and his thoughts. He tells us to write the vision and to make it understandable. I encourage you to take your pen and paper out again, and with childlike faith, make your requests known to God. Take what my mother said, all those years ago, and make it your own; *"I believe in pipe dreams."*

Welcome Home

"Therefore, I say whatever things you ask when you pray, believe that you receive them and you will have them." Mark 11:24

The Spirit of Christmas Past

If I was given an opportunity to look back through a window into my Christmas past, I know I would catch a glimpse of our family driving through town, looking at all the Christmas lights that shimmered underneath snow-covered roofs. I know I would see the Capital building with its' hallways lined with many beautifully decorated trees, each one twinkling in its own right.

If I wipe away the frost from the windowpane, I can see our church Christmas plays being acted out just the same as they were many years ago, and tucked in the background, I can see our families' secret miracle. I remember it so clearly, this particular family needed groceries. My parents took us girls to the grocery store and told us to help fill the buggy! Afterward, dad drove us over to their house, we sat the groceries on the front doorstep, rang the bell and ran to hide. Oh, what fun! They never knew who left the groceries; just that someone cared. My parents always found ways to teach us how to be the hands and feet of Jesus.

Pulling the curtains back to get a better look, I can see my sister and I jumping up and down in sheer delight! It was Christmas Eve, and my dad and mom had just told us girls we would be making the 1200-mile trip south for Christmas! All of my family lived in the South, except for us. Most years, we saw our family in the summer or at Christmas time, but this particular year we were not going South, or so we thought.

My sister and I were like two parakeets locked in a cage, saying, *"Are we there yet?" "Are we there yet?"* I remember our arrival like it was yesterday. The *"weary traveler"* feeling was replaced with anticipation as we stood outside their country home in Tennessee. The smell of hardwoods and chimney smoke still lingers in the air. When my grandpa and grandma stepped outside, they were speechless; only tears and warm embraces followed.

Once the shock wore off, my grandma quickly busied herself with Christmas dinner. Everyone had a place at Grandma's table, with one exception; the children. We had our own special table that was separate from the adults. To this day, it is a standing joke that we have yet to make it to the adult table! Even with kids of our own, we still end up at the children's table.

Oh, the laughter that would roar through the house; glasses clanging and silverware tinkering. Grandpa would be walking around with the video recorder, and Grandma would have the camera taking pictures. Today those home videos and pictures are priceless to our family. Each year a gray jacket of my dad's would get smaller and smaller, and yet he had it on in every home video. We would sit down and watch them for hours, laughing until we cried. How fitting that Charles Dickens is noted for saying, *"There is nothing more irresistibly contagious than laughter and good humor."*

Before Christmas day would end, everyone would gather in the living room to listen to my Grandpa read the *Christmas Story* once again. My Grandpa always made it clear to all of us the reason for the season.

God penned, by his Son, the greatest love story ever told. A Savior was born, who is Christ the Lord. The spirit of our Christmas past has the power to overlap our present, but it will not happen on accident. It must happen on purpose. It is up to us to teach it to our children. I pray this season finds you full of faith and surrounded by family and friends.

In the words of Tiny Tim, *"Merry Christmas to us all and God Bless Us. Every One."*

Welcome Home

"For there is born to you this day in the city of David, a Savior who is Christ the Lord." Luke 2:11

AND FORGET NOT ALL HIS BENEFITS

January is kind of a letdown after a month like December. It is like being asked to follow a stellar talent act. December takes the stage with a standing ovation, and January smells of rotten tomatoes while it holds us, hostage, for thirty-one days!

It is very easy to allow January's uneventful days to cloud our judgement. Instead of seeing the benefits of a new year, we see the loss of an old year.

We have a jar in our house called the *"Blessings Jar."* I took it from the scripture found in Psalms 103:2, which says, *"Bless the Lord, oh my soul, and forget not all His benefits."* I couldn't get that last part out of my mind, *"...and forget not all His benefits."* It is so easy to miss the little blessings all around us. Whether it's in a good laugh with a friend, a cup of coffee bought for a stranger, or just a fun day spent with family.

I remember when my husband's and my first dog died. My heart was broken. My dad called and told me that it was these kinds of moments that marriages were made of. Our society today tries to pacify pain but, the truth is, part of growing as a family will contain some tears. It was around that first heartbreak that I made our *"Blessings Jar."* I didn't want to forget the moments that were gluing our family together. Now, each year, on January 1st, we open our jar and take out the slips of paper and read what made that year special. It is amazing how many benefits we forget!

As I reached in the jar, I pulled out a recent slip of paper that read, *"Water leaked into the camper. Two dogs, a cat, a toddler and a flashlight, not a good combination!"* The story came flooding back to me. As most of you know, our family is living in a camper right now while we relocate. One particular day, I was standing at the kitchen sink in the camper. I had just awakened Eva from her nap. I looked behind me and saw water all over the floor! I quickly cleaned it up, thinking maybe it would just go away. Well, it didn't. About thirty minutes later, it was back! Because it was leaking from underneath the electrical box, I had instructions to shut everything down, including the water, until Chuck could get home. I headed outside, in the dark, to do what seemed extremely simple. However, remember two dogs, a cat, a toddler…and a flashlight.

As I am looking for the waterline, I hear footsteps coming fast from around the camper. I looked up to see Eva running towards me. She had on her panties, a t-shirt too small for her, and rainboots. In her hand, she was carrying a flashlight saying, *"Mommy!" "I'm coming and I got my flashlight!"* Still trying to pry open the box that held the waterline, out of the corner of my eye, I see my cat. She was easing her rather plump body down the camper steps, ready to make a smooth getaway underneath the camper. While this is playing out, our German Shepherd, Maximus, who thinks he is a Police Officer always on patrol, is steady doing laps around the scene. I am praying he doesn't see my cat while I am busy trying to get to the waterline. I finally managed to get into the box, but I couldn't see anything down in the hole. So, I squatted down and leaned in for a closer look. Eva comes right beside me, squats down, and as serious as she can, leans over with her flashlight. It was really hard to take her seriously in panties and rainboots, but I kept my composure because imitation is the sincerest form of flattery.

I finally reached my hand down in the hole and was able to shut off the water. Meanwhile, I felt something breathing down my neck. I slowly lifted my head and was met face to face with Samson, our Golden Retriever. He reminds me a lot of a Politician, always shaking hands and kissing babies. He was literally at my face, and in one smooth motion, he stuck his tongue out and licked my nose, as if to say, *"I am right here if you need me."* I could not contain it anymore. I just started laughing out loud, and then Eva started laughing! I told her this would make the *"Blessings Jar"* for sure!

Life is a series of moments stacked together. Look for them this year and put them in a jar, so you don't forget all His benefits. I promise! They are worth remembering!

Welcome Home

"You crown the year with Your goodness and all Your paths drip with abundance!" Psalms 65:11

You Will Never Make General

I have always been *"Betty Homemaker."* I take after my mother in that department. I enjoy all the domestic responsibilities. The rewards far outweigh the work put in. Outside of the home, my profession takes me to the gym. I am a fitness instructor and supervisor. I enjoy what I do so much that many days I forget I am working. When Chuck and I got married, we decided I would only work part-time, and it has continued to work well for us as we raise our family.

There is no denying it. I am a social butterfly who has never met a stranger. My husband tells me all the time to stop talking to people we do not know. I calmly explain to him that we *will* know them when I am through visiting. My personality works well for me in my field, mainly since I cater to an older population. I have made many dear friends while swapping life stories and day to day activities with them. If you want to know about life, spend some time around the *"old folks,"* they really do know a thing or two.

Helping people live better, inside and out, is what exercise is all about. I have found, many physical problems can be linked internally. What is on the inside of us eventually will show up on the outside. Most people just want a listening ear and a helpful hand. Many of my participants have mentioned how much better they feel after being with friends, laughing and exercising. I heard a quote that I try to make my personal mission every day, *"Be a blessing everywhere you go and leave people better than you found them."*

One morning, as I was getting ready to leave work, I sat down to check my email and finish up some paperwork. I knew once I got home, I would no longer handle any office work. This is something I saw modeled by my dad. It was rare for him to bring his work home from the church office, mentally or physically. He used to say, along with my mother, *"It is all for nothing if we gain the whole world but we lose our family."* As a child, I didn't see the value in those words, but I do now.

As I was sitting there, checking through my email, one of my weight room participants, a retired Military Colonel, saw me. He walked over and made a little small talk. He noticed I was checking my email before I left, and jokingly told me I could do that at home. I told him I tried my best to keep tight boundaries between work and home. I didn't want to spend my time at home distracted by work. At that moment, I saw a staunch man soften and with glistening eyes, he looked at me and said, *"You will never make General that way."* He gave me a wink and moved on. I often wonder if that glistening in his eye that day was one of regret or fond memories? I am guessing probably a little bit of both. It's impossible to raise a family without some regrets, but I hope the fond memories will far outweigh any of them.

A price will be paid, either at work or at home. It is up to us to choose. I made a decision long ago that my family would get the best of me, not what was left of me. I may not make General publicly, but I will be the hero they need privately. I know you are fighting for your family as well. Make sure they win.

Welcome Home

"Remember the Lord, great and awesome! Fight for your families, your sons, your daughters, your wives and your homes." Nehemiah 4:14

EYE OF THE TIGER

I was driving down the road one day, glancing out the window, when I saw an old home-place off in the distance. I could tell in its prime, it had been a beautiful masterpiece, but in its current condition, those glory days were gone. The house was overgrown with shrubberies, vines and unkempt flower beds. The shutters were falling off the windows and the blinds were closed tight as if no one was home. The old shop out back didn't look any better. It was rundown and looked like it would cave in at any moment. Yet, as I drove by, I noticed cars were parked in the driveway. I remember saying to myself, *"How does a once beautiful place get like that?"* I heard these words, *"They quit."*

The Bible says, *"Without a vision, the people will perish."* Proverbs 29:18. This doesn't necessarily mean an instant death but a slow decay; a degeneration in a person's life.

As a new year commences, we are faced with a choice. We can quit and begin a slow decline, or we can continue to make improvements. The second law of thermodynamics states, *"There is a natural tendency of any isolated system to degenerate into a more disordered state."* In other words, anything left to itself will eventually quit.

I remember meeting a lady one time that told me about all the conditions she had and how she was learning to live with her ailments. I did not voice my feelings but I thought to myself, *"What you learn to live with today, you will have to feed tomorrow."* It is no surprise that I never saw this lady again. She quit before she ever got started. I heard Kelly Copeland say, *"We cannot change what we tolerate."* If we tolerate a life of misery, then we will never have a life of pleasure.

One of my exercise classes has nicknamed themselves *"The Huggin Pool."* They are the neatest group of men and ladies, always welcoming everyone with a smile and a hug. Their motto is *"Leave your differences at the door and find something to laugh about."* Life is so much better hung on a peg of laughter. In Alabama, football falls right below church attendance on Sunday morning. And with two SEC teams that play in the state, you are bound to run into football controversy. Here, the colors you wear and the college you graduated from says a lot about the team you root for. However, two ladies come weekly to the *"The Huggin Pool,"* each carrying their water canteens that sport their favorite team. These two ladies sit their archrival canteens side by side and head off to exercise. During their workout, I began noticing they would take a water break at the same time. Wading over and grabbing their canteens, they would hold them up and say *"cheers"* to one another while their team's chant echoed off their lips, laughter covering their differences, choosing friendship over rivalry and deciding not to quit.

A slow decline can show itself in many forms, but there is an eighty-one-year-old gal that defies all odds. She comes each week to an exercise class of mine that is out of the water! One day while we were setting up our mats to do crunches, I watched her get up from her chair and ease her way down onto a mat. I asked her what she was doing since this was very out of character for her? She replied, *"I made up my mind earlier this year. I was going to do my crunches on that mat before Christmas, and I am going to do it!"* She has done just that since then. She says all the time, *"You are only as old as you want to be!"* She refuses to slowly decline.

If time allowed, I would share countless triumphs I have seen with these ladies. I could tell of a seventy-five-year-old lady who, with tears in her eyes, held a three-minute plank and afterward, shared with us how, with the Lord's help, she had beaten cancer. She had a new outlook on life and was determined never to quit. I could tell you of a dear friend who had not taken a flight of stairs in many years. I was privileged to stand there and watch as she grabbed hold of the railing, like it was an old friend, and began to climb step for step.

The prayers I have personally seen these women pray when emergencies would arise in each other's lives are amazing! When limitations try to get the better of them, I watch as friends come alongside one another and let them know they can do it. I stand back and watch a young generation take a stride with the older generation; learning from them instead of pushing them away.

Miracles happen each day to ordinary people but do we stop long enough to notice? Pastor Randy Fuller said, *"A person without a vision is a person without a future."* Vision has sacrifice attached to it, and I see it every day in these ladies. Their everyday decisions reflect their vision. Each week these ladies work with an *"Eye of the Tiger"* tenacity that pushes me to have an unwillingness to quit. They show up when they feel like it and when they don't.

A tiger has incredibly keen eyesight. He sets his mark to aim small and miss small. He will dominate rather than be dominated. A tiger will hit his target every time if... he doesn't quit.

Welcome Home

"Teach us to number our days that we may gain a heart of wisdom."
Psalms 90:12

I Have an Appointment

"He was up before the dawn with his Bible opened up. Seeking truth with every single page he turned. Anyone could see my daddy lived what he believed. With a gentle heart and passion for Jesus's blood…"

-Brian Free and Assurance

Nothing describes my father better. As my sister and I would wake to ready ourselves for school, we would catch a glimpse of Dad. He would be sitting in his chair or standing with a cup of coffee in his hand, gazing out the window, and there it would be, his Bible, lying on the table. This was not on occasion. He had an appointment every morning. My mother was the same. Only, back then, she liked to spend time reading after we had gone to bed.

It was commonplace, in our home, to find open Bibles lying

around with pages of notes laid out beside it. Everyone had a Bible, and we all spent time reading it.

When I grew up and headed out on my own, I slowly began to read less and less. Unraveling typically does not happen quickly, it's a slow fade. It wasn't long before I noticed I wasn't getting very far hanging on the shirttails of my parent's relationship with God. Religion can be passed down, but relationship cannot.

Unfortunately, I found out the hard way that life has a way of demoralizing our convictions without a personal relationship with God. I knew if I was going to succeed, it was going to have to be personal. I had seen it modeled before me my entire life, but until I applied it, nothing would change. The Bible is the most powerful book in the world. It is full of freeing truths that can change any situation, but I realized, unopened and collecting dust, it only served as an ornate piece of religious material that added beauty to my bookcase. It was powerless to stop the hell that screamed wide open in my life.

Somehow, I still managed to convince myself that I was just fine. Jesus himself found time to slip away and commune with God. Yet, I didn't see the need? We are too inexperienced to handle life without guidance. God's word became my guide; my compass. Thankfully, those days seem like a lifetime ago.

Many years ago, when I was newly married, I became so desperate for change in my life that I started to devour the Word and any Christian materials I could get my hands on. One day at a time, I had found a relationship with God, just like I had seen my parents do. It didn't mean instant perfection, on the contrary, but I had found where to go to fix the mess I called my life. It was in the secret place.

Psalms 91 is one of my favorite passages of scripture. It starts off by saying, *"He that dwells in the secret place of the most High shall abide under the shadow of the Almighty..."* I found out that it was in the secret place where I am made whole and learn who I am in Christ. It's in the secret place where I am kept and guarded. It's in the secret place where my marriage is healed, and order comes into my home. It's in the secret place where my patience is refreshed, and my strength is renewed. It's in the secret place where fear has to flee, and peace is still. It's in the secret place where His word lights my path. It's in the secret place where direction is gained for long-term plans. It's in the secret place where success and prosperity for daily living are learned. It's in the secret place where I am corrected and instructed.

Even so, it's only when I *leave* the secret place that application must take place. I now face the many challenges of life head-on because I know WHO goes before me and WHO calms the storm. I know the Lion of Judah patrols the perimeter of my life, and with that knowledge, I walk on in confidence! He is a Friend that sticks closer than a brother and a Father that cares for His children.

Home Sweet Home

I was unwilling to negotiate my time in the secret place but unsure how I was going to manage it once Eva arrived. Nonetheless, I was determined. I knew I was embarking on new territory, and a screaming baby would wait for no one. I asked the Lord to help me and show me the way.

Upon her arrival, I continued with my same routine. I have always been an early riser, and apparently, Eva was too. I am convinced she could hear me breathe. I tried everything so as not to make noise during those early morning hours. I went to some extreme measures! But nothing seemed to work. Until one day, I heard these words in my heart, *"Let her catch you with your Bible opened."* I instantly went and scooped her up! In one arm, I held Eva, and in the other, my Bible. Interrupted as it may be at times, she has learned that I have an appointment first thing each morning.

One particular morning comes to mind. I had just gotten settled down in the peace and quiet with my tea cup in hand when Eva woke up. It was one of those mornings where she needed a lot of attention; if it wasn't one thing it was another. She was crying incessantly. On top of that, Chuck was trying to leave early for work and making all kinds of noise. In a matter of moments, I had Eva on one hip, screaming, with snot and tears running down her face, Chuck asking me questions regarding the day's itinerary, and an empty baby bottle in my all but free hand.

Somewhere back off in the distance, I caught a glimpse of my tea cup and Bible just sitting there. I took a deep breath and looked up at the ceiling as if looking straight into Heaven. I gave a little wink and said, *"I will be back tomorrow, the same place at the same time."* I like to think He just smiled and said... *"Thanks for showing up."*

Welcome Home

"May my meditation be sweet to Him; I will be glad in the Lord."
Psalms 104:34

For Sale: One Used Saddle

To hear my dad describe Mr. Garland Webb is quite a salute to a great cowboy: *He was a gentlemen cowboy, who removed his hat for a lady and his boots in the house. He treated his friends fairly, and his enemies wisely. His neighbors were like family. He was loved by many and envied by all.*

At eighty years old, Mr. Garland was still swinging a leg over the saddle to ride fences and check cattle. He was a cowboy of all cowboys. I needed a saddle, and he had his son's thirty-year-old saddle for sale. I reached out my hand that held a hard-earned hundred-dollar bill. That was a lot of money, back then, for a young ten-year-old girl to save. He reached out his hand and took my money. In exchange, I got my saddle.

My parents taught us by example how to manage money and

explained that it was a tool to utilize, not a master to serve. In our home, money was not given as allowance. It was earned by the work we did. As kids, grumbling and complaining seemed to follow close behind us when work presented itself, but today the lessons have paid off in dividends.

Our parents made sure we had opportunities to earn extra money. We would go with mom after school once a week to clean the hallway and laundry room of Mr. Harvey's apartment buildings. He hired her to clean six apartment buildings, and she paid us to help her. We also would do odd jobs for our dad out at the barn to earn extra money. No matter the job, my folks always paid a fair wage. They wanted us to understand that money was hard-earned. Our regular, daily chores were completed each day, and these were not paid. We were a member of the family and expected to do our part to help.

I couldn't have been more than five or six when we began learning to handle money. Kids are smarter than we give them credit. I remember Dad and Mom explaining to us about the tithe. We were to honor God with ten cents out of every dollar we made. It was to come out first before anything else. They explained how God would always take care of all our needs as we honored him with the money we earned. In my six-year-old mind, I had decided that ten cents out of every dollar wasn't a bad deal; He gets ten cents, and I get to keep ninety. Even at that age, I could see how I came out ahead! After our tithe, we were taught to give some, save some and spend some.

As we grew older and began to hold part-time jobs, our budget grew as well. We had funds in the budget plan such as; car maintenance, gas, insurance, clothes, entertainment and fun things we wanted. My parents were always right there to help direct us, but they were not our personal ATM machine.

When emergencies arose, they were there for guidance, not payment. There were very few times that I could remember my parents paying for an emergency. My parents were raising adults, not children. It was our responsibility to be prepared for emergencies. I can still hear them say, *"The storm is coming, sis! Are you prepared for it?"* When we are prepared for the storm, an emergency simply becomes an inconvenience only.

When I met Charles, I knew I had met my match. I like to describe him as a well-balanced working machine, a cash-only man. I remember thinking, *"Where do I sign to make him mine?!"* We both knew we would never *"get"* without giving to our finances. Wanting something for nothing is like wanting to be skinny while eating a Big Mac. That's upside-down; it's confusion. God never operates out of confusion. He has a system that works. It requires discipline and restraint. But on the other side, it will create responsible, hardworking adults who are productive in society. His system requires me to put my hands to the plow and get to work. Chuck and I knew if we stayed within the guidelines outlined in His word, it would create balance, order and riches in our home.

Mr. Garland has been gone for many years now, but the lesson that saddle purchase taught me lives on. Today, that saddle is almost sixty-years-old with nothing wrong with it that a little saddle butter wouldn't fix. When Eva is older, I plan on telling her the story about how I purchased the saddle she is now riding in. It's a simple lesson with powerful truths. Money comes from hard work.

I pray this principle comes back to her each time she holds out her hand to exchange money for a saddle.

Welcome Home

"Be diligent to know that state of your flocks and give attention to your herds." Proverbs 27:23

DATE NIGHT

We all had our popcorn and coke in hand as we headed in for the show. Our hometown of Pierre had a small movie theatre that everyone frequented. It was so much fun to go see the latest movie that was playing.

As we walked into the theatre to find our seats, I turned to my dad and asked if I could sit in the middle of Mom and him? His response made such an impact on me. He said, *"No Sis, you cannot sit between us. One day you will grow up and have a life all your own, and I do not want to have to get to know my wife all over again."* All those growing up years, we were never allowed to sit between Mom and Dad. Now, sitting beside them was, of course, acceptable but never between them.

My folks have a rather unique love story. They met and

married in three weeks! My father was a young evangelist at the time, preaching and holding revivals at different churches each week. One week he was holding a revival at my mother's church. Dad tells the story that she walked in, wearing a black dress suit, and her long red hair cascaded down her back. He was smitten. Mom says she found her Prince Charming. They spent the week inseparable. He asked her to marry him on Wednesday of that week, and he left on Saturday to go preach a revival in another town. When he returned the following week, they decided not to plan a long engagement but, instead, to elope! They left and went to his folks in Tennessee and were married by my Great Grandfather in my Grandpa and Grandma's living room. How's that for romance?!

When my folks tell their story, people often ask how such a quick love story could produce such a wonderful marriage? Without fail, they explain one factor is a date night. Pastor Tim Brooks of Christian Ministries Church teaches an analogy comparing marriage to a car. Quality time is to a marriage like gas is to a car. It's what makes the car run. The problem isn't that we think our car doesn't need gas. We know it does. The problem is in the thought, *"I think I can make it."* There is great danger in that kind of thinking. A car that runs out of gas takes a lot more work to fix than one that is filled up on a regular basis. Keeping gas in the tank will keep the warning light from blinking on the dashboard.

For my folks, gas in the tank... I mean, date night was on Friday night, and there were some hard-fast rules in place: No children allowed, no unpleasant talk, and no interruptions unless it was an absolute emergency.

I love small-town folks because they are always so predictable. I knew they would be going to Jake's Steak House or, on occasion, to the Outpost for ribs. I also knew the couples that would be going with them. From there, it was off to the movie theatre to catch the latest show.

Every Friday night, I could count on *Brooks and Dunn* playing in the CD player as Mom would be getting ready for date night. There would be a thick fog of hairspray clouding the hallway. It would be so thick you needed a flashlight to see your way through. Dad would be in his pressed jeans, shirt, boots, and cowboy hat, patiently, *"waiting on a woman."* Not much has changed in almost forty years, not even his Stetson cologne.

My folks are more in love today than the day they were married. It did not happen by chance. It was a decision they made many years ago, to be intentional. They taught us girls that we would never drift into a successful marriage. It would take a hundred percent on both sides. To this day, you will find my parents enjoying one another, holding hands, and stealing kisses. They laugh together and sit close to one another. My father still opens the car door for my mother, no matter the weather.

A few years ago, I watched my Grandpa make his way around their vehicle to get my Grandma out of the car. They are both in their eighties, so it took him a little longer than it used to. I just stood there and watched. It didn't take much to see where my father learned his gentleman ways. I couldn't help but ask, *"After all these years, Grandpa, you still get Grandma's door?"* He looked at me without missing a beat and said, *"Sixty-three years! Now, I am not going to say it is the sole thing that has kept us together, but it sure hasn't hurt any."*

I have taken to heart what my parents lived before me. I know one day Eva's Prince Charming is coming for her. I do not want to get to know Chuck all over again. What my Grandpa said to me that day is true. Date night may not be the sole thing that will keep us together, but it sure couldn't hurt any.

Welcome Home

"Catch us the foxes, the little foxes that spoil the vines, for our vines have tender grapes." Song of Solomon 2:15 (Marriage is precious. Handle with care)

I DO

I was standing with my dad on the back porch, over-looking the yard covered in wedding arrangements. I was awaiting the hour that the wedding ceremony would begin. I laid my head on my dad's shoulder and whispered, *"I can't do this."*

The next couple of hours seemed like a blur of emotions. I was a real-life runaway bride. I hid in my parent's bedroom while they tried to figure out why I was backing out. Meanwhile, Chuck was getting ready five miles away with no idea that his bride was getting cold feet.

I was taught love is a decision, not a feeling, but I had been living on feelings for the past five years. I lived for the moment. Instead of making calculated decisions, I did or said whatever I felt like at the time. Chuck was the only constant I had during those years. He always had a plan and stuck to it. Me? I never did. The Bible says in Jeremiah 17:9, *"The heart is deceitful above all things, and desperately wicked; who can know it?"* Jeremiah was referring to our mind, will and emotions.

When we live based on *"how we feel,"* the truth will change daily. True North will not exist, and we will be lost without a compass.

Now faced with a decision that would change my life forever, I panicked. I felt incapable of making such a vow. I had created a mountain of questions and uncertainties because I hastened ahead without seeking God or wise counsel. I found myself empty and on shifting sand. I had planned an elaborate wedding, with no money in the bank, to a man my parents barely knew. Like I said, I lived for the moment. At least Chuck was able to talk me down off the ledge of a large wedding and instead, we planned a very small ceremony in my parent's backyard.

Chuck and I had been dating for five years, but I had kept our relationship a secret from my parents for the most part. I knew there would be hard questions that I was not ready to answer. Not only had I been living a life not marked by a Christian, but I was living oblivious to the fact that there were black and white issues that needed to be addressed. Quality parenting will hit hard issues head-on, but I chose to run from any facts and instead bulldoze ahead without any instruction, only to find it all caught up with me, sitting in my parents' bedroom on my wedding day.

Home Sweet Home

Our society today teaches there are no absolutes, and each person can do whatever they choose and live happily ever after. This works great in fairy tales but not in real life and certainly not in a marriage. God has boundaries He put into place for our success. Marriage is one of those boundaries. Its borders confine it to one man and one woman. The color of skin matters not to God. However, it can be problematic without proper guidance. To ignore race in a marriage will leave you unequipped to handle cultural differences when they arise, and they will arise. Learning the transition from *"His and Hers"* to *"Ours"* can be hard enough. Yet, it is only in the exposure of hard issues that resolutions can be found. My parents knew this. I, however, did not.

My Grandparents walked into the room and found me crying. I had decided I couldn't go through with it and asked my dad to go out and announce to all the wedding party and family that the wedding was off. Immediately, my Grandfather knelt beside me and began to pray for me. It was then that Chuck arrived and saw the commotion. He quickly made his way to where I was and quietly listened as I shared my heart. I expected him to leave after he saw my indecisiveness but instead, he gently said, *"I'm right here, and this is where I am staying."* Through my tears, I saw a man who would love me unconditionally, a man who would not cower when the pressure was on. I knew this was the man my parents had prayed for me to find since I was a little girl. We both were a little banged up with some rough edges, but it was nothing the

Lord couldn't smooth out, given a little time.

I had made my decision. No more secrets. No more living for the moment. I would face my fears and our future together. It would start by walking down that aisle and publicly vowing, *"To have and to hold, till death do us part."*

My father made light of the situation and let everyone know that although the bride had cold feet, they seemed to have warmed up, and there was about to be a wedding!

The guests were due to arrive in thirty minutes, and I had yet to get dressed! Typically, August is a hot, dry month, but for my wedding…it rained a monsoon. Nothing could stop me from getting down that aisle at this point. I slipped my beautiful satin shoes off and laced my arm through my dad's. I was ready.

He walked me through my mother's flower garden on the way to the tent, trying to buy himself a little bit more time before giving me away, but it was no use. He knew I was already reaching for another. Even with my muddy bare feet and a soaking wet wedding dress, Charles was waiting to steal Cinderella.

More often than not, it rains on our anniversary, and we are reminded about what happened that day. It was life-changing. There was a picture taken during our ceremony of us lighting the unity candle. Because of the weather, we could not get it to stay lit. Finally, Chuck tried one more time and got it! I quickly cupped my hand around it to keep it from going out. Chuck followed as well. As we made our way back in front of my father, he said, *"Just as you protected that candle, you protect this flame that burns between you."*

I keep that picture on my mantle as a constant reminder that even though fairy tales may not exist in real life, we still lived *happily ever after.*

Welcome Home

"Above all, love each other deeply, because love covers a multitude of sins." 1 Peter 4:8

There's a Giant Inside

Chuck and I had recently been married, and now we were arranging our new household budget. We had some extra funds and were discussing the best way to use the money. I had some great ideas, but none were practical. Chuck helped to kick in the adult part of me, as he is always very practical, and we settled on the purchase of a new mattress set for our bedroom.

At the time, we did not have a truck so, Chuck called one of his buddies to help him go and pick up the mattress set. As they were about to leave, I opened the door and told Chuck to make sure they didn't forget the tie-downs or bungee straps so the mattresses would stay secure on the ride home. It is an unwritten rule that all good wives holler out last-minute reminders to their husbands, especially in front of their friends.

Home Sweet Home

Once they arrived to pick up the mattresses and got them loaded, Marcus told Chuck to grab the straps so they could tie it down. But Chuck said it wasn't necessary. He figured it would be fine just lying there. For a little added security, he would reach his hand out through the rear window and hold it. So, with that all decided, they loaded up and headed back toward our home.

On the way back, one of the roads opened up, and the speed limit increased, not by much, but enough to make a difference in the wind levels. Without thinking, Chuck lifted his hand to scratch his face. He says at this point, everything happened faster than the blink of an eye, and yet it felt like slow motion. The wind got underneath the mattress and lifted it straight up in the air! He tried to get his hands back on it, but it was no use. It sailed into the oncoming traffic lane. No cars were coming, so they quickly pulled off the road and ran to get it. As they were running, they turned to see a dual pickup truck headed straight for the mattress! To hear them tell it, their eyes got huge, and their spirits were shrinking. They knew the truck was not going to dodge it. Of course, the truck ran slap over our brand-new mattress! As the truck passed and the dust cleared, Chuck and Marcus assessed the damage. Now with a very beaten and battered mattress reloaded in the bed of the truck, they got in, slammed the doors, and Marcus looked at Chuck and said, *"I think we should have used the tie downs."* *"I'm not getting out of this truck when we get back to your house."*

Meanwhile, I was at home getting the room situated for where I wanted the new mattress set to go. Then the phone rings. It was Chuck. I will never forget his words as long as I live. He said, *"Babe, don't be mad. I will fix it."*

When they arrived and hauled in the battered mattress, Marcus lingered back, and Chuck laid it out of the floor for me to examine. My mouth fell open. There on my living room floor lay our brand-new mattress with tire tracks across it! It looked like an over-sized pillow that had gone through the washing machine and then the dryer. It had more lumps in it than poorly cooked banana pudding! My eyes made their way to the bottom of the mattress. I could see the springs popping out. Chuck looked up at me and proudly responded, *"I think I can fix it."* I was absolutely speechless.

I wanted to ream him out and tell him, *"I told you so,"* but as my mind raced through old files of memories, looking for one that gave me the right to blast him…I came up empty. In all my growing up years, I could not pull out one memory where my mother ever talked down to my father. She always spoke to the giant. Even when he made a mistake or didn't listen to her way of thinking. There was never an *"I told you so"* attitude with her. Oh, there were plenty of times she could have, but she always chose to make him the hero. She always built him up and helped him out of whatever pickle they were in. In public or in private, my mother talked fondly of my father, never poking fun or degrading him. To a little girl who often had itching ears, I picked up on it. She made me believe daddy walked on water.

When Chuck and I married, my father gave me some sound advice. He told me to let him be his own man. Give him room to make mistakes.

One of my favorite movies is "Mcklintock." There is a scene where John Wayne is explaining to his daughter, Becky, why she will not be inheriting all his land and fortune. He says, *"But the real reason, Becky, is because I love you, and I want you and some young man to have what I had because all the gold in the United States Treasury and all the harp music in Heaven can't equal what happens between a man and woman with all that growin' together."*

Chuck kept his promise and fixed the mattress. He smoothed out some of the rough spots and tucked the springs back in. He picked the lumpiest side of the mattress to sleep on and gave me the smoother side. When we laid on the mattress, it was lopsided, so we kind of rolled towards the middle. We just decided it was designed that way so we could hold each other close.

For three years, we slept on that mattress and every time I would wash the sheets, I would chuckle as I saw those tire tracks and think to myself... *There is a giant inside.*

Welcome Home

"A soft answer turns away wrath" Proverbs 15:1

A Picture of Happy

One of my favorite things to do is load up in our old Ford pickup truck. We bought it from Chuck's Grandad several years ago, so there is some sentimental attachment to it as well. It's nothing fancy. I am sure you can visualize the type; a two-door pickup truck, with one long seat across the cab, AM/FM radio, the gear shift is still located on the steering wheel, the air conditioner is the hand-cranked windows you roll down yourself, and the seatbelts are buried so far down in the seat, it's impossible to dig them out. And of course, there is the dashboard. It's a little loose from all the wear and tear and has so many photos attached to it. That's my kind of heaven right there.

We load up the dogs, Samson and Maximus, into the back. You would think they were going to a dog's paradise or

Home Sweet Home

something. Chuck can barely get the tailgate down before they are flying in with their tails wagging in full swing. If you haven't heard me describe *"the boys"* before, let me fill you in. Samson is a Golden Retriever, and Maximus is a German Shepherd. Maximus is the Police Officer, continually patrolling and protecting, and Samson is the Politician, always shaking hands and kissing babies.

Once we have the dogs loaded, we all find our place in the cab of the truck, and Chuck cranks 'er up and revs the motor three or four times. Then we go, off flyin' down a backroad somewhere, windows wide open! Eva is squealing with delight, and the boys are leaned so far over the sides of the truck, their tails are all that remain in the back of the truck. Everyone is having the time of their lives! All you have to say in our home is *"TRUCK RIDE!"* and everyone is scrambling to go.

I am reminded of one such day, we were just rolling back into town from one of these truck rides, with a little ice cream to go with it, then I remembered I needed a couple of things from the grocery store, so Chuck wheeled us in and parked. We had just gotten out of the truck when a gentleman walking inside the store stopped and held up his hands as if looking at our family, our dogs, and our truck through a movie screen and he said, *"Now family, I'm gonna tell you somethin' right now; If "HAPPY" had a picture next to it this would be it."* He smiled and continued walking on, shaking his head.

It doesn't take a lot of money to build fun memories. It only takes a little time and lots of laughs. My folks taught us girls as we were growing up that *"life"* was done together as a family. My father never bought us kids a bicycle. He bought the whole family bicycles. They knew we were going to grow up, but they refused to let us grow apart. They prepared for the future when we were young, and we had a wonderful time because of it.

Build your memories. Find your *picture of happy* and make it something your family remembers forever.

Welcome Home

"That this may be a sign among you when your children ask in time, what do these stones mean? That you will answer them and say… these stones shall be a memorial to the children of Israel forever." Joshua 4:6

The Ride

Some horses are just born for kids. Mr. Ed was one of those horses. My folks named him after the TV show *"Mister Ed."* He whinnied all the time, so they felt it was a very appropriate name.

One afternoon, Dad was finishing up some work out at Mr. Harvey's barn, and I was riding bareback in the round pen. I decided to speed Mr. Ed up a little bit, and without giving it much thought, I kicked him into a trot. At six years old, Mr. Ed was a lot of horse bareback, and I could not hold on very well, especially going in a circle. As he started to trot faster and faster, I began to lose my grip more and more. It only took seconds for me to meet the gate head first and then land in the dirt.

When I gained composure, I noticed I was on one side of the pen, and Mr. Ed was on the other. He just stared at me as if wondering what I was doing down there? I immediately began to cry, and daddy came running to my rescue. Rescue seems like a pretty strong word when referring to Mr. Ed, but at six-years-old, those scrapes and bruises seemed as big as he was. My dad scooped me up and dusted me off. He put me in the truck and took me home to Mom. She bandaged up my scrapes and laid me down for a nap. I remember when I woke up, my dad came in and sat down beside me. He began to explain to me how I could not let one fall keep me from ever riding again. He told me that if I let fear win now, it would conquer me later in life. He finished by telling me we were going back to the barn.

I didn't want to go, but I knew there was no way out. Dad loaded up the family, and we headed out to the barn. I noticed Mr. Ed was still corralled instead of turned out to pasture. Dad knew all along that we would be going back. He helped me get on Mr. Ed's bare back, and the same as before, he had me trot around. I gripped as tight as I could, and to my surprise, I didn't fall off! Sometimes experience really is the best teacher.

Years later, this lesson would play out again; only this time I would be riding a three-year-old colt. I usually did not get to ride the young colts, but Red was extremely gentle. One day, I got too comfortable and threw my leg over the saddle horn to relax. I decided to take off in a lope while in this position. It spooked him and he took off in a wide-open run with me on him. No amount of force I applied could stop him. I knew this was a dangerous place to be.

Our dad had warned us girls about runaway horses. They run blind, not caring what may be in their way. I knew Red was heading straight for the barn. The only problem was we were about a half a mile away on a gravel road, and there was a lot between us and the barn. I quit trying to stop him and just held on. He rounded the first turn and was headed for the second, which would make a straight shot into the barn, but when I saw where he was aiming, I knew I would have to bail off or risk serious injury. His aim was for a small side door in the barn. I did the only thing I could do. I jumped! I slid for what felt like miles, and then all went calm. The worst was over except for the injuries I incurred. It took me several weeks to heal, but as soon as I was able, I put on my boots, walked out to the barn and saddled Red.

Now that I am grown, I can see that my father was not teaching me how to get back on a horse. He was teaching me not to fear the ride of life. Life will throw us off sometimes. We must learn how to shake off the mud, dust off the dirt, and climb back in the saddle again. When I got back on my horse that day, I still had the scars, but I left the fall behind me. I refused to carry the weight of all the dirt and mud. The fall is not what defines us, it's the ride.

I decided a long time ago no matter what life would throw my way, I would love wide open, I would laugh loud, and I would live salty, as I heard a young man say, flavoring all I come in contact with. I want to leave this world a better place. I cannot do that from the dirt. When life bucks me off, and it will at times, I will let tears wash away the dirt and grime. I will let relationships be a part of helping me swing a leg back over the saddle again, and most importantly, I will not carry what was never mine to carry.

Fear, regret, loss, grief, sadness, anger, hurt, sickness, disease, and poverty. Jesus paid it all. He nailed it to the cross so I could go free. My mother has a beautiful quote she says all the time, *"Life was made to be lived, not feared."* So, saddle up, it's going to be a beautiful ride...

Welcome Home

"Surely, He has borne our griefs and carried our sorrows, yet we esteemed him stricken, smitten by God, and afflicted. But he was wounded for our transgressions, He was bruised for our iniquities. The chastisement for our peace was upon him, and by his stripes we are healed!" Isaiah 53:4-5

Good Night, Sweet Dreams, I Love You, I Will See You In The Morning

"Good night, Sweet dreams, I love you, I will see you in the morning." No words could have fonder memories to me. I have heard them said a thousand times, and without fail, they have never brought disappointment.

In our home, eight o'clock was bedtime for us girls. It used to make us so mad. We would moan and groan because we wanted to stay up! But my folks knew 6 AM would come early for school. For the most part, bedtime was strictly observed in our home. It was without negotiation and regard to the season. This was not only so we would get a good night's rest but also so that our parents could have some quiet, uninterrupted time together.

This can be easily overlooked, and yet it is so important. Time with our spouse is valuable. Whether it is simply to review the day or just to enjoy each other's company. It must be shielded from the element's life will wield. Structure and schedule are the building blocks upon which success will hang in any area of our lives, marriage included.

My mother was a Southern Belle who kept to her southern roots even as far as South Dakota. Her make-up, hair and nails seemed to always be perfect, and yet she could weed a garden, clean house, and work beside my dad as if perfume and sweat were a match made in heaven. When we were little, our mother did not work outside the home, so she found side jobs to earn extra money, like selling Mary Kay. As we grew older, Mom worked in the school system as a teacher's aide at Washington school in our small town of Pierre. This allowed her to still be on our schedule.

As a child, I never realized her strategy, but today I am very thankful for the sacrifices she made. I rarely came home from school to an empty house. Her presence made all the difference. There must have been many dreams she laid aside to make sure we knew the value she placed upon her home and family. She planted seeds in my sister and I that have bloomed in our own families as we continue in the same manner.

I can still remember opening all the lipstick samples that would come in the Mary Kay boxes. We loved to watch the

Home Sweet Home

house fill up with ladies ready to try on the new products and leave with beautiful faces. Without much warning, the parties began to pull Mom away. Instead of everyone coming to her, she was now going to them. This meant Mom was absent during the evening hours, which, of course, entailed supper and bedtime routines. It did not take her long to see this was not going to work for her.

Even though they needed the extra money, nothing was more important to my mother than making sure she was home where she was needed the most. In exchange for Mary Kay, she began to clean apartments for Mr. Harvey. She would clean the hallways and laundry rooms of six apartment buildings. This was the perfect set up for her. It allowed for her to make her own working schedule and for us to tag along.

Before Eva was born, I worked a few evening classes a week without giving much thought to it, but when Eva arrived, those evening classes were coming around too quickly and were wearing not only on our evening routine but on our marriage as well. I remember one day I finally had enough. I could see the strain it was putting on everyone. I told Chuck this had to change, and he agreed. We began to pray for the Lord to open up a door. It wasn't too long after that conversation that the opportunity presented itself for me to rearrange those hours to early morning instead.

I knew there was something more important I had to do.

There was somewhere more important I had to be. My family was counting on me. I had a husband who needed my time and a little girl who was waiting for me to tuck her in and read her a story. There were bedtime prayers to pray and precious words I did not want to miss.

As I turn out her light each night, I can see her nightlight glowing on the shelf. It is the same one that glowed on my dresser as a little girl. I can't help but drift back to all those nights as a little girl myself, remembering stories my mother would read to us girls, as well as being tucked in and kissed by my parents, knowing they would be right downstairs if we needed them.

I can still remember some nights right before Brittney, and I would drift off to sleep. We would hear Dad and Mom yell up the stairs, *"PAJAMA RIDE!"* We would leap out of bed, and they would load us up for a late-night ice-cream trip in our pajamas! We thought it was the best thing in the world as little girls. No amount of Mary Kay was worth missing this.

Standing there, watching Eva tucked in with Mr. Elephant, I could see it all playing out again. As I gently bent down to kiss her forehead, the words come rushing back to me, and I softly whisper one more time, *"Good night, Sweet dreams, I love you, I will see you in the morning."*

Home Sweet Home

Welcome Home

"I will both lie down and sleep in peace, for you alone, Oh Lord, make me dwell in safety." Psalms 4:8

MAKING OFFERS ON MEMORIES

I am by no means a garage sale junky, but on a beautiful day when the sun is shining and the birds are chirping, I enjoy loading the boys (dogs) in the back of the old truck and driving around with Eva looking at what people are selling. You can find some really neat things on occasion.

I remember one day before Eva was born. My folks were in town, and we decided to peruse around and see what we found. There was one house that was lined with cars, so we figured it was a good place to stop. The lady who owned the house was selling everything in her husband's shop. It was a gold mine for men. My dad was lost in a sea of tools, and my mom and I were looking around at some home decor items when I ran across a shelf that held souvenir spoons. I collected souvenir spoons and needed a shelf to hold them. My mother and grandmother both collected them as well, so it was only natural that I would collect them. I asked the lady how much for the shelf, and she told me. I paid her for it and was about to leave when I realized the shelf still had her spoons attached. I told her I would remove them so she could keep them. It was then that she looked at me and said, *"No. I do not need them. Those are past memories. My husband and I had a wonderful life together. He died last year, and I am just cleaning out his old shop and all of our stuff that I no longer need."* I just stared at her. I didn't know what to say. My mind flooded with something my dad had told me a while back as we were leaving a different garage sale. He said, *"We do not realize that we are making offers on memories."*

A couple of days later, I was cleaning the shelf and removing all the spoons. When I finished putting them in a bag, I took them to the garage and opened the trashcan to throw them away. After all, they weren't my memories. They held no significant value to me, but at that moment, I froze. I couldn't do it. I looked back down at the bag, and this time I took notice. On each spoon was written a different location or destination. There were more cities and states than I could count. My eyes got a little glossy. These were all of her spoons that she had collected over her lifetime, and I was about to toss them away as if they were meaningless. The thought of the lives lived behind these souvenir spoons stopped me in my tracks.

I went back inside and found my car keys. I knew right where she lived, so I headed towards her house. I parked my car out in front and walked up to her door. I knocked. She answered. I explained who I was and why I was there. In more words than I can remember, I told her garage sales are full of dusty junk and old worn-out clothes, but some things just don't belong. These spoons were one of them. I told her I was about to throw them away, but I just couldn't do it. I had to return them. These were her memories. The spoons may be made of a cheap silver-plated metal, but a life is made by precious moments stacked, *"one by one."* Memories may be black and white, but life is lived in color.

As I left that day, I felt a little funny making a big deal over some spoons, but were they really just some spoons? Each one was attached to a special place in time.

I will never know what she did with them after I left. She said she was going to get a shadow box to put them in. I hope she did. I hope she placed it somewhere she passes by often when walking through her house, and maybe, on occasion, she will remember a young lady who was unwilling to make offers on memories.

Welcome Home

"I thank my God in all my remembrance of you, always in every prayer of mine for you all, making prayer with joy, because of your partnership in the gospel from the first day until now." Philippians 1:3-5

The Finish Line

The feeling of excitement rushes over us at the start of something new; a new baby, a new house, a new job, a new puppy, or perhaps a new dream. Our willingness to work hard is a solemn promise we vow. However, as the new wears off and the bathroom still needs to be scrubbed, and the now full-grown dog still needs to be walked; our pace begins to slow.

    Chuck and I watched this play out when we bought our first house. It was in a beautiful neighborhood. Each house was custom built to suit the new owners. So much potential lay on each empty lot. However, we quickly realized, for most people, it was only a change of address. There was no change of mindset. I am a walker/runner. So, each day as I would head out for my exercise, I would watch new people moving in. I was so excited at all the new neighbors I would be meeting and friendships that would be kindled. Until I started to notice the garage door go up, the car pull inside, and the garage door come down; the blinds were pulled tight, and the doors were locked. On occasion, I would catch a glimpse of the garage as someone would be leaving, or I would catch a quick glance into the home as the front door was left open by young kids running out to play.

It was in these small glimpses that a thought occurred to me. The outside of a house may look amazing, but it's what is on the inside that shows who we really are. Sounds a lot like us doesn't it? It's only when an unexpected guest stops by that the clutter, dirty dishes or dysfunction can easily be marked. We can mask it by a garage door and tightly closed blinds, but it sends a clear message to those around. The finish line was forgotten.

There is a scripture in Proverbs 24:27 that reads, *"Prepare your outside work. Make it fit for yourself in the field and afterward build your house."* This spoke volumes to me the first time I read it. I had to learn to put first things first. I had to take care of what was necessary, like my kitchen sink, the laundry and my family relationships. Then I could take care of what was comfortable, the extra stuff. I found out it is in a daily schedule that busy can be eliminated. This is the only way to keep my home and relationships running smoothly. God outlines a perfect plan for success in His Word. It's a plan that brings order, not confusion, structure and not disarray.

Home Sweet Home

A few years back, I ran a 5k race. I have always loved to run, so on occasion, I enjoy friendly competition. I was physically ready for the race but unprepared for the adrenaline and excitement. These are elements that training could not prepare me for. When the gun went off, so did I. I was set for a six-and-a-half-minute mile. My friend, who was running with me, backed off, but I kept the pace. I thought, this was a breeze. After all, I ran a mile all the time for a quick workout.

About the time I hit two miles, my pace was slowing, and my mind was winning over my legs. I wanted to quit, but I knew I couldn't. When I passed the third-mile marker, here came my friend, breezing past me. I had nothing left. She had remained steady. I, on the other hand, started too strong and had nothing left for the finish. When I rounded the last turn, I could see the finish line. One would think that would be the most invigorating part, and it is, but it is also the most exhausting.

My heart was racing. My lungs felt as if they were going to burst, and my legs felt like limp dish rags as well as concrete cinder blocks all at the same time. Yet I could hear the crowd cheering me on, and I could see the finish line flags waving. In the crowd, I caught a glimpse of my husband and little girl. Eva was on daddy's shoulders, and they were screaming and waving.

In that split second, I changed my thinking and demanded my body finish this race. I switched to a gear I did not know I had left. My biggest fans were watching, cheering me on. They believed in me. My mind had to win the race in order for my body to follow. It wasn't enough for me to simply cross the finish line. It was how I crossed the finish line that mattered to me.

Our children will not remember all the money we made, but they will remember the times we threw a pole in the water or built a fort in the living room out of old blankets. Our spouse will not remember every *"I love you"* said, but they will remember the times we valued them over the phone. Our friends will not remember every text message sent, but they will never forget a drive across town to just sit on the porch and visit. Our homes may not be perfect, of course not, they have people in them. However, when things are picked up and put away, when the vacuum has been run, and the clothes have been folded and neatly put away, well… a clean home just *"lives"* better.

Our lives are spent with the finish line in sight. God isn't concerned with how we start as much as He is with how we finish. When your heart is racing and your lungs are ready to burst. When your legs feel like limp dish rags, remember your family is watching, cheering you on. They believe in you! So, run your race and finish well.

Welcome Home

"I, wisdom, will make the hours of your day more profitable and the years of your life more fruitful." Proverbs 9:11

LIKE ARROWS

My parents never did for themselves what they didn't do for the whole family. If one night a week was set aside for date night, then rest assured, one night a week was set aside for family night. It was Thursday night, to be exact. We had a coffee cup that had little strips of paper in it. It was full of fun ideas like going for ice-cream at Zesto's, swimming at the YMCA, watching a movie, bike riding or horseback riding. We had family board games to choose from or other seasonal activities.

My sister and I took turns picking from the cup each week. Family night was just a fun time of laughter and being together. It was another non-negotiable in our home. It happened every week, and we were expected to have chores and homework done so we could participate. Having time together as a family created a bond that could not be broken. It built a bridge that allowed us access into each other's lives and this bridge would extend through time.

I will never forget when Eva was just a baby. My father said to me, *"Chuck and you have eighteen years to raise Eva. There will be a lot of things vying for your time. Put the BIG rocks in first. Let everything else fall where it may."* The BIG rocks consist of Faith, Family and the Fundamentals of being a productive member of society. It can be easy to let tiny pebbles become the most important thing and then wonder why there is no room left for the BIG rocks. We took his advice to heart and went to work.

Children will develop based on the parenting we deliver, not the friendship we offer. I never did understand that until I had a child of my own. My folks were not my friends. They were my parents.

In the Bible, David compares children to arrows. In order to create an arrow that will cut through the wind as it flies, it must spend some time on the chiseling block. Psalms 32:8 says, *"I will instruct you and teach you in the way you should go. I will guide you with my eye."* One definition of the word *teach* means to shoot in a straight manner. An unwrought piece of bone or rock will never be hewn into an arrow that cuts through the wind just sitting beside a chiseling block.

I once had a lady tell me that she didn't have to worry about her children's Christian upbringing because the Christian preschool was doing that part for her. I told her that this was our problem in society today. We are letting someone else do what was intended for us to do. We live oblivious to the teaching our children are receiving as we roll through the carpool line.

Our Pastor made a statement one Sunday morning that resonated with me. It hit me right between my eyes as I heard him say, *"If I ask your children who is the Godliest man or woman they know and if your name, as mother and father, does not roll off their tongue, you are failing as a parent."*

God holds the parents responsible for the upbringing of their children; not grandparents, teachers, daycares or preschools; not churches, Sunday school, friends or the state. Although all of these play an important role in the training of children, the ultimate responsibility rests on the mother and father. Particularly the father, whom God has appointed *"head"* to lead and serve the family (Ephesians Chapter Five).

In ancient times, just as today, the arrow has three parts. These parts include the arrowhead, which is the destructive part. Also, the body, to carry the arrowhead. Lastly, the tail designed to keep the arrow on course. Many arrowheads were made from bones or rocks. They also learned how to heat metals to extreme temperatures and pour the liquid into molds for shaping.

Because my parents held my feet to the fire and spent time

molding and shaping me, I can honestly say they are two of my very best friends today. Our times together are full of joy and laughter, activities and fellowship. I look forward to being around them. This does not just happen. No family just arrives at a harmonious outcome. It is chiseled at four, molded at eleven, and heated at sixteen. It is left to harden and then removed from the mold by actions, not just words until all that remains is a perfectly shaped arrow ready to fly and hit its mark. As the bow is pulled back and the arrow is ready to be released, know this, an arrow will only fly as far as the one holding the bow. When the bow is released and the arrow takes flight, cover it in prayer and watch the Lord's precious hand guide it through the years.

I am so thankful for my mother and father and the atmosphere in which I was raised. It wasn't condescending, destructive or critical. It was an atmosphere that was rich in encouragement and held tenderness, love and patience.

If your story doesn't look like mine, that's ok. That's the beauty of God. Your story isn't over. He gave you blank pages so you can write a new chapter; a chapter about a life you dream for your family. Title your new chapter, *"Family Night,"* and watch the pages fill. I promise! You won't be disappointed!

If I only had a few short sentences to leave Eva, I would say what Erwin Raphael McManus penned to his children.

Home Sweet Home

Eva,

"You are the tip of the spear. You are the future. This is your fight. I pulled the bow back as far as I could and gave you all the strength I had to send you into flight. Fly far and true. Cross enemy lines. Hit the mark. Set captives free. Keep striking until the battle's won."

I Love you BIG,

Mommy

Welcome Home

"Like arrows in the hand of a warrior, so are the children of one's youth." Psalms 127:4

Waving Palm Branches

It was Sunday morning, Palm Sunday. I knew we would tune in to our church service online of course, but my concern wasn't for *my* spiritual walk. My concern was for my little girl who could not understand why we no longer were gathering together at Church.

She didn't understand not going to Sunday School, with all of her friends, to praise and learn about Jesus. That settled it. I had made my decision. I called Eva to me and said, *"Eva, I want you to go get all of your stuffed animals and line them up. Get ready, Girly, we are going to have Church this morning, Eva Style."* I wish I could have captured the look of excitement on her face. She ran down the hallway and began gathering every animal and lined them up in the living room.

I started collecting Bibles, an offering bucket, and the arts and crafts. Daddy's job was the music. Once everything was set up and ready, Eva got her little stool and sat with her animals. Suddenly, she jumped up and ran to get her purse. She unzipped it and started passing out coins to all of her animals. She wanted them to have an offering to give that morning.

I asked Eva if she was ready for church, and there was an unquenchable squeal of *"Yes!"* I had the service scheduled. There would be Bible action songs, offerings, lesson time with a puppet show, and even an arts and crafts section! I treated this Sunday just as if we were in her Sunday school room with all of her friends.

As the songs began, Eva jumped up and we all participated in *"Father Abraham"* and *"I'm In The Lords Army."* Memories came flooding back as we sang and danced. Daddy decided to pull out the dart gun during the song *"I'm In The Lord's Army,"* and every time we said, *"Shoot the artillery,"* he would shoot out a dart. Eva squealed with delight!

When our song service was complete, we prepared for the offering. I talked with Eva and all the animals in attendance that morning about giving and why we give. Daddy queued the song in the background, and while Ron Kenoly sang *"Give to the Lord,"* Eva took her cup and walked around collecting the offering from all of her animals and from Mommy and Daddy.

After the offering was gathered, we moved into the lesson

where Daddy took the lead and read from Eva's picture Bible. He read to her all about the triumphal entry! While he told the story, I sat behind the couch with Oliver the Donkey and Mr. Elephant,(Don't ask me why the donkey's name is Oliver or why there was an elephant in the room...I have no idea...Just go with me here). They said they came to tell Eva what the city looked like on that special day, so many years ago, when Jesus rode into Jerusalem. Oliver and Mr. Elephant told her all about the people waving Palm Branches and saying, *"Hosanna!" "Blessed is He who comes in the name of the Lord!"* By this point, she was standing up, with both hands in the air, shouting, *"Hosanna,"* right along with Oliver and Mr. Elephant.

After the puppet show was complete, it was arts and crafts time. We prepared to make our very own palm branches from construction paper, tape and popsicle sticks (skillfully crafted).

Once we were finished, it was time for the parade! We lined up to wave our palm branches at Jesus and shout, *"Hosanna!"* I quickly snatched up the living room throw blankets. I used one as a sash on Daddy as he played Jesus, and the other two I threw over Eva's head and mine. While trying to set the scene, it probably looked more like a bad representation of *"Robin Hood"* than of Bible characters, but it worked.

As Jesus came walking down the aisle, holding Oliver the Donkey, Eva and I waved our Palm Branches saying, *"Hosanna! Blessed is He who comes in the name of the Lord!"*

Home Sweet Home

We were laughing until we couldn't catch our breath, which caused me to realize something. I don't want to miss out on wonderful opportunities to pour into my family while waiting for the perfect moment to arrive. The greatest ministry we will ever have, happens within the four walls of our home. It is here that families see the resurrection of Jesus lived out. Perhaps our Sunday school church service that morning makes for a better blog than it looked in real-time, but it lived loud.

Resurrection Day, (Easter) is coming whether we are gathered in our beautiful churches or not. It is coming whether my family has on their new Easter attire or not. It is coming whether or not my extended family gathers for baked ham, corn casserole and carrot cake. It makes no difference. There is an empty tomb and the day must be celebrated!

Don't miss *"waving palm branches"* (Even if made from construction paper) waiting for the perfect opportunity for a lesson. Embrace the moment you're in, and carry on your traditions as best you can. I can assure you; it will be an Easter you won't soon forget.

If you find yourself reading this post, wondering who is this Jesus I speak so passionately about? I would love to introduce you to Him. It is as easy as asking him to be Lord and Savior of your life. He will resurrect in you, that which you thought was dead. Religion can never offer what relationship can. Religion is like a heavy stone one has to carry around, while relationship walks with you hand in hand.

Let Jesus walk with you this Easter. He is waiting.

Welcome Home

"I am the resurrection and the life. He who believes in me, though he may die, he shall live. And whoever lives and believes in me shall never die." John 11:25-26

LIVING ON BORROWED TIME

I was in town one day and saw a familiar face. I waved and greeted her. I asked her how she was doing. She responded with a heavy sigh and closed eyelids, *"I'm just living on borrowed time."* I just stared at her. I wanted to laugh, but I held it back. There was nothing wrong with her at all. That was simply how she responded to life in general. She reminded me of Mariah Popham in *"Summer Magic,"* where she says, *"Now, I like to believe in a cloud that's a first-class cloud. Thick and black clean and through.... I always expect the worst, and I ain't ever been disappointed."* There could not be a better description that fit this lady. It would be easy to overlook one rather important detail in my encounter. Her daughter was standing right beside her, listening to how her mother responded to life. Unbeknownst to her, her mother was teaching her how to speak.

I read a wonderful story in Judges that clarifies my point so well. Judges 12:6 says, *"They would say to him, say "Shibboleth,"* and he would say *"Sibboleth," for he could not pronounce it right..."* In short, the Gildeadites used the pronunciation of this word to recognize fleeing Ephraimites. The Ephraimites had a different dialect when pronouncing this word. They said it with a soft "s" sound instead of a stronger "*sh*" sound. Because of this, their speech would give them away, and Israel could recognize their enemy.

When we speak, it doesn't take long for others to recognize what we believe. Faith is always tested in the soil of uncertainty. Our response determines the outcome. Faith is an inward confidence and assurance. Faith will take God at His word when circumstances seem to deny the truth. I love what my husband says during football season when an Alabama player makes a touchdown, and he attempts a showy performance. He just shakes his head and says, *"Act like you have been here before."* Fear will react, as if it has never seen a problem. Faith, on the other hand, will act like it has been here before.

There is an interesting fact about an empty plastic water bottle in an airplane. Upon the airplane's dissension, it will crush because of the change in the cabin pressure. However, a full plastic water bottle will not crush under the change in pressure but remain the same. Is it possible that our actions resemble that of a water bottle? Do we crush under pressure and react out of fear? Or does the faith that is on the inside of us keep us from crushing under the pressure?

Every time Eva sees a rainbow, she hollers out, *"Look!" "It's God's promise!"* Not only does she see hope, but she also speaks hope. Her speech gives her away. It's as if she never saw the storm that produced the rainbow.

Chuck and I do not teach Eva to deny the rain, but simply to believe the promise attached to the rain. God said there would be trouble, but in Psalms 91, He promised that He would be with us as we GO THROUGH the trouble.

Our Nation is going through a storm. There is no denying that. Let's trust in God's promises. No longer looking at the rain, but rather, looking for the rainbow.

Welcome Home

"We are hard-pressed on every side, yet not crushed; perplexed, but not in despair." 2 Corinthians 4:8

GATHER ROUND FOR PRAYER

When my sister and I were little girls, our dad would wake us up each morning to a peppy little medley he had creatively added lyrics to. Picture Frank Sinatra swaying to the tempo of Big Band music, singing these words…

> *"Good morning, it's a beautiful day. Good morning, time to start on your way. Good morning, I've got something to say. Good morning, good morning to you…"*

It is quite comical looking back, but growing up, it used to make my sister and I so mad! I can remember the rush of those early mornings all too well. Dad was the breakfast cook while mom would ready herself for work as a teacher's aide. Brittney and I would slowly get ready for school ourselves. Once we were finished, we would quickly sit and eat our breakfast before grabbing our backpacks and heading off for school. It all sounds like clockwork unless you have lived it.

I can still hear my dad yell down the hallway in a silly tone, *"Ya'll come gather round for praya,"* and my sister would echo back, *"Praya."* It became a family joke as the years went by.

Our morning prayer together was never anything long, but it had a lasting impact. It always covered thankfulness for another day, protection in our daily activities, and the ability to learn and accomplish what was set before us. The hustle and bustle of quick breakfasts, packed lunches and forgotten book bags can quickly take center stage while prayer finds itself lost in the shadows.

Prayer must be intentional and without excuse. My dad told me something a few years back that I never forgot. He said, *"Too many Christians want a Gospel they are not accountable to and a grace they are irresponsible for."*

One day, not too long ago, Eva and I were outside. She was riding her bike, and I was jogging. I turned into the driveway before she did. I thought she was right behind me. As I turned to circle back around her, I saw a car approaching slowly. We do not live on a busy road, in fact, it is a dead-end road. Nonetheless, the car was slowly approaching, and it scared Eva. She jumped off of her bike and ran to the driveway screaming, *"Mommy!"* I quickly scooped her up. I thanked the lady for driving so cautiously as kids played on our road all the time. She smiled and said she was so impressed at how Eva jumped off the bike and ran to the curb, just like we had taught her to do. I too, was thankful the instructions were followed.

Later that day, as we were doing other things, Eva stopped and said to me, *"Mommy, Jesus stopped that car today. He saved my life."* I looked at her as I caught my breath and said, *"You are exactly right, Girly! He did!"* She was never in any real danger. The car was not moving swiftly, but… it could have been. It could have been someone who wasn't paying attention or someone busy on their phone, not watching where they were going.

Many years ago, I spent my days in fear, begging God to watch over my family and myself. I lived in constant unrest, waiting around every corner for something to go wrong. I was unequipped to handle life and all its obstacles. With my dad's statement ringing in my ears, I realized the responsibility was mine. I picked up my Bible and began learning of the power it possessed. I found out that I didn't have to beg God for anything. Sitting around wringing my hands and pleading with God wouldn't keep danger away. Protection is a promise that belongs to every Christian but left unchecked, it will sit unclaimed. Today, my family gathers around for prayer, just like I remember doing all those years ago. Where I once lived my life in fear and turmoil, I now live in peace. Knowing the promises of God will see us through whatever we may face.

Home Sweet Home

If perhaps you find yourself where I was, I want to encourage you today. God is not angry with you. He does not stand ready to bring His wrath upon you or your family. He is a loving Father who has precious promises wrapped up in scripture to encompass your life.

I wrote this prayer several years ago. I pray it over my family often. I hope it is a blessing to you as much as it has been to me…

"Father, we give you thanks for this day, and we declare your loving-kindness each morning. We ask that you watch between each of us while we are absent from one another. Guard our going out, and our coming in from this day forth and even forevermore. Give your angels charge over us to keep us, for we abide under the shadow of the Almighty. We thank you that as we gather back together this evening, we will find nothing amiss in our household, and we will declare your faithfulness each evening. You are the Lion of Judah, and You patrol the perimeter of my life!" – Amen

Welcome Home

Psalms 118:24

Genesis 31:49

Psalms 91:1,11

Psalms 92:1-2

Psalms 121:8

Job 5:24

April 27th, 2011

It was 5:15 pm. A mile-wide tornado was heading straight for us. It moved like a combine tractor out harvesting wheat. Only in this case, it was harvesting lives, possessions and property. It was impossible to see one end from the other. Dad had called to warn us when the newscasters realized this deadly tornado had turned and was now headed straight for the heart of Tuscaloosa. It was headed for my mother and father's heart as well.

On the other end of the phone line, my dad was met with hysterical screaming. The tornado was already upon us. Chuck had the phone in his hand and heard my dad say, *"Please, take care of my girls."* All went silent…

It was a typical spring day here in the South. The sun was shining, and the birds were singing. This particular spring day was

Home Sweet Home

unusually warm and felt more like July than April. The town was going along with business as usual. We had been warned that it would be a day marked by strong storms and possible record-sized tornadoes. My sister and I had just gotten back to our apartment that we shared downtown. We were roommates during our college days. Chuck and I were dating at the time and I decided to call him and ask him to come over.

The storms were fast approaching, and I was a bit uneasy. I had also called my mom and dad to get their thoughts on the weather. My dad was always one for skepticism when it came to storms. He made light of the situation and said, *"Well Sis, back the car out of the driveway and pour anything that looks like sin down the drain."* Basically, implying I needed to get my life together. I laughed and hung up the phone shortly after. Had I known that would be the last time I would talk to my dad before all hell broke loose, the conversation may have gone a bit differently.

The minutes that followed would drastically change me forever. We heard the warning sirens sound for our area. The course for this monster they called a tornado had changed, and it was headed straight for us! We quickly huddled in the bathroom with a mattress over our heads. My eyes became the size of saucers as I heard it approaching. I thought to myself, *"What is that sound?!"* The sound of an EF5 tornado placed markers in my eardrums that I will not soon forget. The sound lies somewhere between that of a Boeing 747-jet airliner preparing for takeoff and a railway train engine speeding down the tracks.

Everything began to shake. The barometric pressure became so intense it pinned us down to the floor. Our apartment building exploded, sending bricks, wood, glass and other debris flying through the air. Outside our apartment, you could hear the sound of cars, trees and people taking flight on a ride not requested.

As debris was flying through the air and our life flashed before our eyes, I remember thinking, *"I am not going to die today!"* Determination is a key ingredient in survival of any kind. A Psalm came to my mind that my mom had taught me growing up. She used to quote it every morning during our morning prayer. I lifted my head and began to quote Psalms 91 as loud as I could. In that moment, it was as if something dropped into the room with us. Like someone draped a covering over us and time stood still.

When we knew it was safe, we made our way out of the bathroom and sifted through all kinds of debris to get to the front door. It was jammed, so we climbed out of a shattered window onto what used to be our balcony.

It's hard to put into words what we saw. How could something that lasted about thirty seconds leave such life-altering destruction? This jet-propelled train engine left a path 314 miles long and devoured everything that dared stand in its way. I thought my eyes were playing tricks on me as I stared into

Home Sweet Home

destroyed homes of perfect strangers. It was as if my childhood dollhouse had become life-size.

I could see people crawling out from under the debris, climbing out of bathtubs and calling out for help from second story buildings. We could hear the cries of people trapped underneath houses as we ran up and down our neighborhood, trying to help as many people as we could.

It was impossible to get in or out of the area. All the roads were blocked by downed trees and power lines, disheveled cars and buildings. People were walking around covered in blood, tears and dirt, in utter shock and hopelessly lost. No one knew the extent of the damage until the days that followed. All that was known was it went on for miles. The sound of sirens would become a lullaby we would sleep to, if we slept at all.

Many weeks later, as clean up and restoration began to find its start, I found myself back at our old apartment. Nothing remained inside the building. It was empty and lifeless. As I was getting ready to leave, I ran into the owner. She was doing some evaluations of the building. We talked briefly and then before I left, she shared something so interesting with me. She told me that the apartment building was the only building in the neighborhood that would not have to be totally demolished and rebuilt. She said the contractors came out and told her that although it would need to be completely gutted and reconstructed, the foundation was solid.

I knew at that moment what the Lord was trying to show me. There was nothing wrong with my foundation. God simply had a major reconstruction project to do in my life. Whatever my past rebellion, upon coming to Christ, a practical reinstatement of God's word as the governing principle for my life had to take place. Without change, I would compromise the level of life He desired for me. I knew God was turning my heart back toward him and welcoming me home.

There was a story that made the morning paper about a little boy separated from his family during the tornado. They were out eating, and the restaurant took a direct hit. First responders found the boy in the kitchen freezer. When he was reunited with his parents, they asked him how he managed to get into the freezer? The boy replied, *"The man with wings put me here."*

People often ask me if I live with great fear of tornadoes since that storm. I tell them honestly that I do have a great respect for tornadoes, but I do not fear them.

Although I didn't see him, I felt him. The man with wings covered us with his feathers that day and under his strong and mighty wings, we too, took refuge.

Welcome Home

"He that dwells in the secret place of the MOST HIGH shall abide under the shadow of the Almighty. I will say of the Lord He is my refuge, my fortress, my God and in Him will I trust." Psalms 91:1

A Place to Call Home

Traveling from place to place can be so exciting. There are always new sights to see and sounds to hear. At every turn, there are new people to meet. This is exactly what my folks did in their early years. Home was hitched behind them as they traveled the United States as Evangelists. At one point, they had two babies riding in the back seat of the pickup truck. Brittney and I were very young during those years, but I do have a few flashes of memory from those times. For all of us, pulling into a campground and setting up camp was home. We would get to ride our tricycles around while dad hooked up the necessities outside the camper and mom worked on the inside. An evening fire and picnics were common place. My sister and I slept in the back of the camper in our pink bunkbeds with heart covered sheets. Ruffled curtains hung on the windows that matched the sheets. In the little snippets that I remember from those early years, we were having the time of our lives.

My folks were traveling out west for several revivals they had lined up, when they passed through the town of Pierre, South Dakota. My mother told me in a letter she had written to me, *"As we passed through the city of Pierre, it just felt like our roots were here, it felt like home."*

When your growing up years feel larger than life, it's hard to imagine another place could ever be as wonderful. As Mr. Harvey, a dear family friend has told my folks many times, *"Home is where you raise your kids."* I knew I had to find it. I didn't want to miss out on the greatest adventure of my life, just drifting. Aunt Bea, in *"The Andy Griffith Show,"* says it perfectly, *"Well, I guess that's how it is with these drifters. They get the urge, and they go. Pity they're so restless, unable to stay in one place for too long. They miss so much."* I don't want to be a drifter. I want my family to smell the same smells coming from the kitchen. I want them to hear the same creaks in the floor. I want them to know what it feels like to have neighbors that feel like family. I want Eva to know the same porch light that flickers at dusk. That can only happen in a place where your roots are allowed to run deep.

Still, the thought of the unknown is intimidating. Familiar will keep you trapped if you let it. Familiar will disguise itself as safe, responsible, and stable. None of these are bad qualities. In fact, without them, our lives will never be all they were created for. Erwin Macmanus said, *"Although you are grounded in your past, you must not be grounded by your past."* Knowing when to settle is a skill that has a fine line between quitting and finishing. When you know what your life is about, it will have such a profound impact on the decisions that you make. It will show you which ground to give up and when to press on.

Somehow, we get the impression that dreams look like big white fluffy clouds, and we simply jump from cloud to cloud, embracing our tomorrow with no obstacles. But the truth is, some of those clouds have rain in them; lots of rain. I had to learn, no matter what, rain or shine, the only way to tomorrow was through today. God was ordering our steps, not our miles. I doubt seriously if anyone would have blamed us if we had settled and just quit. Living in an empty house, a camper, and an apartment made us feel more like nomads than dream chasers. Living out of suitcases and battling one obstacle after another makes a person begin to question what they believe to be true, but there was something in Chuck and me that wouldn't let us quit. We just knew the long-awaited promise was going to become a reality, and it finally did.

As we drove to a new state, a new city and pulled into our new driveway for the first time, it was a moment I will always remember. It was just like my mom said, *"It felt like our roots were here. It felt like home."* There was nothing spectacular about it for anyone else, but for us, it marked the end of a fifteen-month journey. The finish line was crossed as a family. There was so much excitement shown from the three of us—each in our own way. We never noticed that it was pouring down rain during portions of the day, which just seems to be God's stamp of approval for us.

The first morning waking at our new house, I sat in my front porch rocker listening to the sounds of a woodpecker off hammering in the trees. I heard an owl making his last hoot before the sunrise. I could hear the leaves rustling and the creek gurgling by. I watched a lonely traveler make his way down the road.

Just before dawn was about to break, I looked up and saw my porch light flickering. I couldn't help but smile. I pray it's the same porch light Eva lives by her entire life, knowing she better be home by the time it's turned on. I pray it's the same porch light that her daddy turns on when her date brings her home for the first time. And without question, if she ever loses her way, I pray it will be the same porch light she follows home.

A house is just a shell. It's the people inside that make it a home. For that reason, I plan to leave a trail a blind man can follow. I will find a closet to mark up with inches grown each year. I will spend my time mopping hallways where muddy feet have run past and covering the refrigerator with artwork. I plan on placing family photos throughout the house as a timeline to follow.

I will make sure our roots run deep here with hard work and diligence to the task at hand. Laughter and tears will leave their mark on our new home. When Chuck and I are old and gray and our time comes, whoever lives here after us will, without question, be able to say, the Howard's truly lived here. It was the place they called home.

Welcome Home

"And they found rich green pastures and the land was broad, quiet and peaceful..." 1 Chronicles 4:40

It'll Wash

No one should ever see a grown woman driving through town slurping down a child's squeezy applesauce. No mother should ever have to lock herself in the closet in order to eat the last slice of cheesecake in peace and quiet. And yet, I am embarrassed to say, I have done both.

I never knew growing up on a small ranch would help me in the child-rearing arena. When Eva was a baby, changing diapers felt more like branding calves than motherhood. Some days, as a mother, locating a hairbrush to calm the mess and clothes that do not have finger-paint stains on them, can seem to be unattainable goals.

Driving down the road with a two-year-old IN YOUR LAP because she has shoved cat food so far up her nose and it is now located somewhere in the nasal passageway will have you frantically trying to get to the nearest doctor. A set up like this will make any mother feel less than gorgeous.

I remember when Eva was born. It upset my schedule and organization; my way of doing things. No one bothered to tell me life was no longer going to be about me. Oh, I guess people did, in their own way, but it never fully registered. I remember one day I was so frustrated that things were not perfect. There was always something to wash, dry and fold.

I shared my feelings with a dear friend, who is an older lady. Her response changed my view permanently. In her Portuguese accent, she said, *"Stop worrying about the house so much. The baby is going to grow up, and the house will still be here, with all the laundry and dishes to go with it, but the baby will be gone."* Truer words have never been spoken to me.

Life was about someone else now. She showed me in that statement how to give and serve someone else other than myself. We are all selfish by nature. Anything that disrupts what we deem as normal becomes a nuisance.

Being a mother has taught me that I will never "get" without giving to it. It is in giving that we receive. It is where we find fulfillment.

Raising a family and making sure they have what they need is the highest calling of any mother. It sometimes can be a very thankless position, but it is an irreplaceable role that God gave to a mother.

Handprints all over the walls, dishes piled in the sink, toys scattered from here to yon, and a husband that desperately loves you makes being a wife and mother simply perfect. I have learned that clothes are made to get dirty, and houses are built to be lived in. After all, it'll wash.

The cleaning and the scrubbing will wait till tomorrow,

For children grow up, as I've learned to my sorrow.

So quiet down cobwebs, dust go to sleep,

I'm rocking my baby, and babies don't keep!

Welcome Home

"Her children rise up and call her blessed; Her husband also, he praises her." Proverbs 31:28

Pen Pals

I have heard it said many times that it is only after a person is gone that we share what they mean to us. Why we do this, I do not know. I, for one, do not want that to be the case in my life with people that I love. I want them to know how much they mean to me while they are living.

My cousin, Lindsey, and I were talking on the phone one day this past week. We were laughing and crying over memories from our childhood trips to our Granddaddy's. She made the comment that her kids, AJ and Addison Jewel, were pen pals with him. I thought that was the sweetest thing, and it got me to thinking about all the letters he has received through the years and still does. His children, scattered all over the United States, writing to keep him up to date with their lives and updating him on the grandchildren, and now great grandchildren. Of course, filling him in on the latest accomplishments, from extracurricular to scholastic. Oh, the memories that pass over pen and paper. We never realize the history we are writing.

As I sat thinking about pen-pals, I realized what I needed to do. Sometimes a person needs a trip down memory lane. Sometimes a person needs to know how much they mean to you. Sometimes a person needs to know how they have impacted your life.

I pray as I write my letter, you, dear reader, might see someone in your own life who needs reminding of just how special they are. Never take people for granted. After all, people are what life is all about.

Dear Granddaddy,

You have always been a simple man; a man of the past. It doesn't take much to make you happy; a thickly sliced tomato sandwich with mayo and good ole white bread or sitting on a porch swing listening to it rain. Perhaps traveling down an old dirt road with a country store at the end of it, or meeting a young gal, named Bessie Jewel, at the "Snow Frost" in town. That was Heaven for you. The love you have for your family goes without saying, and you treasure the times we gather together and share stories of the present and the past. These simple pleasures are high class living for an old country boy like you.

Hotdogs are a gourmet delicacy in your house, with Nutty Bars for a sweet ending. A box of Shipley doughnuts carries more memories than it does pounds for our family. There is no place that can make a doughnut better than the old bakery in Greenwood. I can still feel the chocolate filling run down my face as it gushed out of the sides. A little coffee to go with our cream and sugar made the doughnuts perfection.

Three little girls lined up beside you on the front seat of that old car of yours. I think it was a Montecarlo or Impala. Either way, we didn't care much. We were lined up singing, "Sweet Potato Pie and Shut My Mouth," While you drove us around Greenwood. Eva Jewel now sings the song as loud as she can. Only, it's from the front seat of an old pickup truck. Both of your great-granddaughters are named for the young gal at the "Snow Frost."

What fun we had as little girls, traveling to see you each summer; swimming at the city pool, and playing games with our cousins. You would take us to the park to watch the hot air balloons sail off in the sky. Mom and Dad always made sure each summer visit had family reunions to attend and watermelons to eat.

Growing up with you as our Granddaddy was something special. Nothing gave you more heartwarming pleasure than your children and grandchildren. You should know, your simple life has rubbed off on us all in one way or another.

There is now a new generation waiting to learn about Shipley doughnuts, "Sweet Potato Pie," and Nutty bars. We all have more letters to write to you. So, keep living and enjoying the simple life. The *world has been a better place because of you.*

We all love you BIG,

Welcome Home!

"And now these three remain: faith, hope, and love, but the greatest of these is love." 1 Corinthians 13:13

Getting My Hands Dirty

Growing up, the only thing I ever really dreamed about was being a wife and a mother. I loved teaching so, playing school and dress up came very naturally for me. Most of the time, I pretended I was my mother, always wearing her dresses, heels, and jewelry around the house, or I would pretend to run errands in her car as if I was going somewhere under the carport.

To me, she was perfect in all her imperfections. She made everything extra special. She always dressed so beautifully, and her hair and makeup seemed to always be done just right. She would make me feel like the number one kid in school when she would come to eat lunch with my friends and me. She never missed a field trip as a designated driver. She always made sure to bring special birthday treats to school, so I had something to share with my class, and of course, the icing on the cake was when she would take me out of school to go to the beauty shop.

Oh, what fun! She always made it a big deal. She made sure the appointments were separate so, Brittney and I each got time with her all to ourselves. We would always get a bag of chips and a coke while we got our hair cut or, in those days, permed! Looking back, I can see my mother was always right in the middle of whatever was going on. She was never afraid to get her hands dirty.

I used to catch myself picturing, what I thought, the perfect mom looked like: the perfect clothes, the perfect mom hair, the house in perfect order, the family involved in the perfect activities, and the kids dressed to perfection. I took one look in the mirror, and reality slapped me in the face.

I also took a look around at our home. I noticed perfection had long ran out the door; order remained, but they do not make toddler toys to go with the color scheme of any home!

I was further brought to reality when I looked down at Eva, and she was barefoot, covered in dirt, and holding a great, big juicy worm up for me to see. The bow in her hair had long been thrown somewhere in the house. I couldn't help but laugh to myself.

For me, putting up laundry, cooking supper, planting flowers, and making mud pies doesn't exactly work with perfect nails, hair and expensive shoes.

On one episode of *"The Waltons,"* (which is another favorite show of mine) Olivia Walton, the mother, attends choir practice at Church. She has decided she needs to be more involved in things outside the home. At the end of Choir practice, all the ladies stay to have tea and socialize. Olivia quickly realizes she doesn't fit in.

One of the choir members slides over by her to visit. Olivia makes the comment that she needs to get going because her husband will need his supper. The lady leans in and whispers to her, *"Don't worry, the more you socialize with us, the more your husband will learn to make his own supper."* It took Olivia all of two seconds to get up and leave. When she got home, she told her husband she found more joy in caring for her family than standing around gossiping with those old ladies.

I like to think the writer was trying to teach us as mothers to get our hands a little dirty within our own homes. Thomas Moore says it perfectly, *"The ordinary arts we practice every day at home are of more importance to the soul than their simplicity might suggest."*

For me, I have never regretted my decision to get my hands dirty. I do not want to be an ornament draped in my home that simply observes life being lived. My mother never took me to the park and watched me swing. She was the one pushing me, higher and higher.

Home Sweet Home

It's funny, I find she still pushes me higher. She encourages me to always be the heart of my home; enraptured in every mess, in every lesson, and in every hug. There will always be a special grace that exists for the season we find ourselves in as mothers. Live it to the fullest and get your hands dirty…

"I don't want to drive up to the pearly gates in a shiny sports car, wearing beautifully, tailored clothes, my hair expertly coiffed, and with long, perfectly manicured fingernails. I want to drive up in a station wagon that has mud on the wheels from taking kids to scout camp. I want to be there with a smudge of peanut butter on my shirt from making sandwiches for a sick neighbors' children. I want to be there with a little dirt under my fingernails from helping to weed someone's garden. I want to be there with children's sticky kisses on my cheeks and the tears of a friend on my shoulder. I want the Lord to know I was really here and that I really lived."

– Marjorie Pay Hinckley

Welcome Home

"Honor her for all that her hands have done, and let her works bring her praise at the city gate." Proverbs 31:31

LIFE IS JUST BETTER IN THE COUNTRY

A close friend of mine told me once that life was better in the country. That is, of course, if a person enjoys solitude and wildlife that occasionally wanders by. One evening, not too long ago, this very thing happened. A curious critter decided to do just that, wander by. Some people bless a new house with a housewarming party- not the Howard's. We prefer to let a smelly skunk spray his ominous odor on our house.

I was sitting in the living room with Eva when we heard what sounded like a hissing cat. I jumped up and quickly ran to the front door and opened it to see what was going on. I couldn't get it closed fast enough. The undeniable fumes of a skunk filled my eyes, nose and mouth while the smell drifted past me and settled on everything in our living room. Eva piped up and said, *"Pew Yew!" "Mommy, what is that?"* I am sure you are familiar with the old saying, *"Curiosity killed the cat."* Well, it didn't kill us, but it sure did Christen our dogs, front porch, living room, and, yes, yours truly! The dogs took the initial hit, but the aftermath seemed to be just as bad.

Chuck came waltzing down the hallway shortly after and asked what in the world happened! I explained that in his short absence, a scene from *"The Night of the Grizzly"* had just played out. He just looked at me for a minute before saying, *"Next time you hear something, and you feel the need to look, please wait before you open the door."* I was pretty sure I was about to be sleeping on the couch with the odor I carried. Perfume, candles and fabric freshener were not masking the smell in the house or on me at all. Every time I sneezed, I had the unpleasurable reminder of the opened door.

The next morning it was very easy to see how the scene had all played out. All we had to do was follow the smell. The dogs must have gone to greet the passerby and were met with a very unwelcoming spray that not only landed on them but inadvertently the house and humans. I can see it now, Samson, with his patriotic personality trotting right up to introduce himself and Maximus following behind, telling him to wait until he has secured the area. The points of contact on both dogs confirmed my theory.

There is a solution that is basically vinegar and baking soda that helps remove the skunk odor. The next day, we spent a beautiful morning washing down the dogs with *"Skunk Shampoo."* Eva thought she had hit the jackpot! I strapped rubber gloves on her, and she went to work. We waited several hours for the boys to dry in hopes they would smell better. We were denied. There are some things only time can take away. A skunk smell is one of those things.

Unfortunately, we were not finished hauling loads from the storage units to the new house, so that afternoon, we had the pleasure of making a three-hour ride with the boys in the back of the SUV. We got Eva buckled into her car seat, and Chuck and I took our places in the front; windows cracked and a can of Febreze in hand. Then, off we went. We were loaded up like the Clampetts. I couldn't help but chuckle to myself as I thought of my friend's words. Life was and still is better in the country!

A few days ago, I had just finished making breakfast, and I noticed it was pouring down rain outside. How I longed just to go sit and enjoy the rain on my front porch, but moving boxes seemed to keep appearing. We had accomplished so much in a very short time, but the list of "To Do's" seemed to keep growing. My dad had told my mother one day, not too long ago, *"It's not the workload you will remember when your old and gray, it's the moments you took time to stop and enjoy the rain."* I quickly called for Eva and told her to grab a blanket and come with me. We went out on the front porch and curled up in the rocking chair and just watched it rain. Samson laid under my legs, creating a nice footrest, and Maximus stood guard next to us, per usual.

The skunk smell is long gone from the porch now, and only an occasional reminder whiffs up from the boys. What seemed like a catastrophe, bubble-wrapped in inconvenience turned out to be a memory we will laugh about for years to come.

Eva will not remember all the moving boxes, the U-Haul trips back and forth, or my list of "To Dos," but she will never forget, we stopped long enough to enjoy the rain.

Welcome Home

"You will show me the path of life. In your presence is fullness of joy; At your right hand are pleasures for evermore." Psalms 16:11

Swimming Lessons

Chuck and I have never been big on extracurricular activities for Eva while she is so young. For us, until Eva can decide, on a deeper level, the activities that she really enjoys, we will jump, run, kick, flip, and dance in the yard. There is one ability, however, that we thought to be more of a necessity than extracurricular; that was swimming lessons. We both love water and spend a lot of time around it. Whether taught by a professional or by us, we wanted her to know how to float and be able to get in and out of a pool, if needed.

Eva was two at the time, almost three the following month. We had a place in town that taught toddlers the basic water lifesaving skills, so we signed Eva up for a four-week course of lessons. I was the designated shuttle, and Chuck was going to come by as soon as he got off work. Eva was so excited when she saw the water and all the kids!

There was a calm before the storm, a storm I never saw coming. When her session arrived, the instructor took her from me and walked her over to where they would be getting into the pool. I sat down on the side to watch. We were told, as parents, we could stay as long as our child didn't start crying or reaching for us. If the instructor couldn't gain control, we would have to leave and watch the session from behind the glass. As soon as Eva figured out I was not coming with her, the storm erupted. She screamed and tried to climb away from the swim teacher. She was reaching for me as if it were her last lifeline. The director came over to me and asked me to please go out behind the door in hopes that Eva would calm down. My heart was heavy, but I did as I was asked.

Eva was in unfamiliar territory, scared, and with someone that she did not know. Although I could see her, she couldn't see me. The screaming only got worse when I left. My heart was getting heavier by the second until I could not take anymore. I burst through the door and went up beside the pool and asked them to hand her to me. Before I was able to grab her, the director came up to me and asked if she could give me a little advice before I pulled her out of the pool. I conceded. She said, *"Would you prefer tears of the unfamiliar or traumatic tears because she doesn't know how to get out of the pool?"* She continued with, *"I will let you take your child, but if you take her out of this pool, you will be teaching her that Mommy will save her every time she is in trouble. This is not just a fun activity you have signed your child up for. This is to save her life if she ever needed it."* She finished by saying, *"I am asking you to go back out behind the door and give us a chance with her."* With tears streaming down my face, I turned around and made the longest walk I have ever made back out of the pool area and left my little girl screaming for Mommy. It seemed so painful at the time, but I know now, the pain was a long way from her heart.

Chuck told me, later that day, in not so many words, *"Our job as Eva's parents is not to suffocate her but to give her wings."* To do that, it means, in some cases, walking away. Standing behind the glass, I realized that was the first time I had ever had to let her go. I knew I had done the right thing, but no one can prepare you for how it feels.

A lady was sitting across the pool who had witnessed the whole thing. She walked out to where I was, behind the door, and simply hugged me. A complete stranger and yet, a common thread woven between us; motherhood. She let me cry on her shoulder. She understood exactly what I was feeling. Her child was a couple of years older than Eva, so she had some experience under her belt to offer me. I am thankful for her kindness to me that day.

All of our endeavors as parents are moving us toward the moment of release, and yet it's the hardest part we face. So many

Home Sweet Home

thoughts race through our minds, wondering if we have deposited the right things into them for success. As hard as letting go is, watching them fly is the greatest joy a parent can have.

I found out that day, swimming lessons don't always happen in the pool.

Welcome Home

"Jesus grew in wisdom, stature and favor with God and man." Luke 2:52

THE GRILL

As I stared out the kitchen window, looking at the old grill standing guard like a silent sentinel, I thought to myself, *"What does your vantage point to the sights and sounds which occur in the backyard look like old friend?"* You have been a bridge over troubled waters and a refuge for my family. Light-hearted laughter and conversations float on the sound waves around the patio.

Watching Chuck pour charcoal into your belly and seeing the flame ignite the coals is pure pleasure for me. The amount of charcoal stacked in our garage is uncanny. It leaves a mark that clearly defines Chuck's favorite place to be. I know you have heard the phrase, *"Daddy, wait for me"* more times than you can count. Eva is like her mother. She doesn't want to miss the smoke encompassing the barrel or the smell of charcoal as it is first being lit. There is nothing like the smell of your coals burning to perfection. It penetrates the atmosphere and leaves anyone within range coveting the next few hours. Even the boys sit salivating for their choice cut of meat to fall. At three-years-old, Chuck has already taught Eva that no fancy utensils are needed, a simple fork will do just fine. He believes the closer a person gets to what they are grilling, the better the quality.

For any grill master, a few key ingredients must be present, one of which is the right seasonings. Eva runs to grab her stool and races across the kitchen floor, sliding her stool in front of her. She climbs up next to her daddy as he takes out his seasonings to rub them on the tender cuts of meat. Eva pipes up and says, *"Ok, Daddy, now, what do we need?"* The second ingredient contains two-parts that go hand in hand, time and patience. If you rush through the grilling process, you end up with meat that is done on the outside but under-cooked on the inside. Grilling has an astounding resemblance to parenting if one looks closely enough.

It's not until our trusty friend's coals are a dusty-gray with only a faint red glow that Chuck knows it is now time for the deliciously seasoned cuts of meat to be placed on the grill. From the grandstands of the kitchen, I can see him pick Eva up while he lifts the lid to the grill. The smoke rushes to find its exit. Eva is so excited to watch her daddy flip the meat. She watches carefully as he shows her what pieces need to be moved around.

He always gives her a job that makes her feel so important. I can hear the excitement in her voice when she runs inside to tell me that daddy needs his cup with the sauce mixture in it. She carefully takes it back outside to him. I can see his *"grilling fork"* principle playing out in more ways than one. Being a father from a distance will never produce the quality in our children that close encounters will.

Chuck's heart was captivated the day he became a father. At his first glance of Eva Jewel, he was smitten. I have watched a gentle giant become subdued under her spell. Her tiny teacups seem so small in his hand. Nonetheless, he enjoys every sip at her tea parties. He grins from ear to ear as he watches her run across the yard in her Elsa play dress and church shoes, all the while looking for Mommy. *Hide and Seek* with Chuck is like trying to hide *"Clifford the Big Red Dog." Yet,* the squeals of excitement coming from Eva are like trumpets of triumph as she finds her daddy hiding behind a tiny basket. But it is the night-nights when she whispers in his ear, *"You are my prince, Daddy,"* that I love the most.

To master the art of grilling is one thing, but to master the heart of a father is another. When the screams of a little girl can be quieted by the protective arms of her daddy or fears of the dark vanish because time has been taken to teach her the power of a flashlight, it becomes easy to see the markings of a father. To watch him kneel down beside her bed and teach her to pray makes my heart skip a beat.

I have been blessed to have two such wonderful men in my life, my own father and my husband. Any father would pray their daughter would marry a man like him. He exemplifies the characteristics of a father and executes his role with duty. He is a defender when he has to be, disciplinarian when he needs to be, and provider because he is called to be. Eva Jewel is one blessed little girl, and I make it a point to tell her so. I have always thought my own father walked on water. Eva doesn't know it yet, but one day she will feel the same.

Welcome Home

"Children's children are the crown of old men, and the glory of children are their fathers." Proverbs 17:6

SUGAR AND SPICE AND EVERYTHING NICE

It is evident, in watching Eva Jewel grow, that she will never bend her head but will always look the world straight in the eye. She has sheer determination about her. I can see it even at three-years-old. My mother says she is very strong-willed. It reminds her of another young lady she knows. She told me, *"Not to worry, teach her how to harness it, and the finished product will turn out wonderful."* It would be this characteristic, alongside God's merciful hand, that would bring Eva Jewel safely into this world.

It was my sister's birthday, June 27, 2016. I was stopping by her office to surprise her. When I arrived, we chit chatted and laughed at how pregnant I looked. I was due in two weeks, but my C-section was scheduled one week prior to my due date. I made mention about the uncomfortable *"Braxton Hicks"* I was having. She jokingly said, *"Wouldn't that be funny if you were actually in labor!"* Turns out, she was only off by one day; one miraculous day!

There was not much change throughout the evening. The contractions were still regular and now, somewhat intense, but I kept brushing them off. Around midnight I woke up as if someone had jolted me awake. I began to time the contractions. They were precise and defined. I called my doctor, who encouraged me to wait a few more hours to make sure. Since it was my first baby, she knew I had plenty of time, and she did not want me to make the one-hour drive to Birmingham for a false alarm.

By five o'clock AM, the contractions had intensified a great deal. My mother and father wanted me to go to the hospital right away; they both sensed an urgency. I, however, was unsure. I was two weeks early from my due date, and I knew most first-time mothers tended to be late. With so many confusing thoughts racing through my mind, I finally stopped and prayed. I heard the Lord gently speak to my heart and say, *"GO."* That was all I needed.

When we arrived in the doctor's office, they took me straight back. It did not take Dr. Routman long to see that I was definitely in labor. They wheeled me over to *Labor and Delivery* and hooked me up to the monitors. I was rescheduled for a c-section that afternoon. Chuck had gone upstairs to get us registered. My mother stayed with me until Chuck returned. I was in severe pain by this point and started to cry.

Within the next few minutes, things started happening very quickly. My nurse became very concerned while looking at my monitor. She immediately flipped me over onto my side and got in my face. She said, *"Your baby is having trouble breathing." "I need you to calm down, focus and take deep breaths. I am going to get the doctor."* She left out of the room in a dash! Moments later, Dr. Routman came into the room. I started crying again and begged her to get my little girl out safely. She comforted me by saying, *"Don't you worry. We are simply going to have an early birthday party right now!"*

It felt just like the movies. I was flying down the corridor with the nurse's staff in a full sprint headed for an emergency delivery. The anesthesiologist met us in the delivery room. He said to me very seriously, *"There is no time for an epidural. I have to do a spinal block."* Which meant, one chance; no room for error. I grabbed the nurse's hand and began to pray. There was no delay; in seconds, I heard the most glorious sound I have ever heard. Eva Jewel was crying.

Meanwhile, my mother was able to track down Chuck and let him know that I was having an emergency delivery. He left everything in registration and came quickly to surgery. The nurses suited him up swiftly, and believe it or not, he entered the room the moment Eva Jewel entered the world. Talk about perfect timing!

Later, with family all gathered around to welcome our new arrival, Dr. Routman came into the room to check on us. My dad made it a point to ask her, *"Exactly how much time was remaining for Eva Jewel?"* Dr. Routman solemnly said, *"Less than an hour."*

My placenta had torn off the uterine wall, and Eva Jewel was suffocating. There was no way to know this until I was hooked up to the monitors, which is what my nurse took notice of. Had I not gone into labor two weeks early, we would have lost our precious *"Jewel."*

For the majority of these cases, when the baby is removed, he or she needs immediate oxygen and usually other medical attention. Miraculously, Eva's oxygen levels were perfect, even after going twenty-four hours in dire straits. Dr. Routman said she breathed a sigh of relief when she heard Eva Jewel's strong lungs. We left the hospital in two days with a healthy baby girl in our arms!

Months later, I came back for my check-up appointment. I was walking back to the examination room when I saw one of my nurses. She had tears in her eyes as she shared, *"I was walking up and down the hallway praying for Eva Jewel and you."*

The pivotal moments surrounding Eva's delivery are more than I can recount in this short story, but it taught me that ordinary heroes are everywhere.

Back in the examination room, my doctor examined my scar. She apologized because it was not perfectly straight. I mulled this over in my mind as I was driving home. The accuracy of my scar could not have bothered me less. It's our imperfections that show people the beauty of our story.

Never be afraid to show people your scars. We were not meant to be victimized to the past but victorious in our future.

We will celebrate Eva Jewel's fourth birthday in just a few days. She is an inquisitive little girl. She often asks me how God makes little girls? My mind reels with all the things I could tell her, but none seem good enough. I simply stroked her face, recalling the day, not very long ago, when the nurse laid her in my arms. I just smile and say, *"Eva Jewel, little girls are straight from Heaven. They are made of sugar and spice and everything nice."*

Welcome Home

"And to the Lord belong escapes from death!" Psalms 68:20

The Fourth of July Parade

Without question, if you took each family member of mine and asked them separately what was the *"highlight holiday"* during our growing up years, each one would say the Fourth of July! All holidays were celebrated in our house, and each one carried its own special traditions. However, the Fourth of July was just something extra special.

Many years, my Aunt Jeanne and Uncle Reggie would come up to Pierre, South Dakota, for their summer vacation. Usually, they would plan it around the Fourth of July. Brittney and I would be itching with anticipation for their arrival because they had two boys, Gary and Brian. All of us kids' stair-stepped, so we were all right around the same age. We would have such fun playing out at the barn, riding horses, or going with the family to tour the Capitol building or the Oahe Dam. Sometimes we would even make the 2 ½ hour trips to Mount Rushmore.

Nothing, however, could top the Fourth of July Celebration. The preparations would start well before daybreak. Dad spent his time loading up enough horses for everyone to ride, while Mom would be busy in the kitchen frying chicken, making potato salad and icebox lemon pies. I can still see the old green cooler sitting there, full of ice, awaiting delivery of all the homemade goods (my folks still have that old cooler and use it to this day- if only it could talk).

Once the adults managed to get all the supplies, horses, and kids (in that order) loaded, we headed out to the annual Fourth of July Parade! Our town parade was a sight to behold. It had all the floats, old cars, firetrucks, tractors, and lots of horse and buggy teams. Many years my dad would take our team of horses and let people fill the wagon. I can still hear my dad say, *"Walk up, Ed."* Mr. Ed would let his buddy do all the pulling if he could get away with it.

What made our parade extra special was the horse and rider section it offered. Each rider carried a flag of one of our fifty states. If you're concerned about our country in any way, I encourage a trip out to South Dakota. They still bleed Red, White and Blue out there.

It was always so fun to ride horses in the parade with our

friends and watch all the people line the streets. I could always spot my mom and Aunt Jeanne, sitting on the back of Mr. Harvey's truck, waving to beat the bands!

When the parade was over, we all rode our horses into the fairgrounds. It wasn't a far ride from where the parade ended, and it was our job to stake claim to the big cottonwood tree while we waited on Dad to get there with the truck and trailer. Then Mom would set up the picnic! It would be a day filled with picnicking and rodeos!

There were always two rodeos, an afternoon and evening one. Us kids would spend the day riding around the fairgrounds catching only glimpses of the afternoon rodeo while the adults caught the details. Then, all would quiet down for a few hours, and you could see people spread out on blankets napping or tending to their horses awaiting the big event.

The evening rodeo was always a packed grandstand. Dad would back our wagon up to the fence, so we would all have a front-row seat to the rodeo. There were so many exciting events to look forward to! There was barrel racing, calf roping, goat tying, saddle bronc, and bull riding! Truth be told, everyone was there for the bull riding. It was the most anticipated event of the rodeo, for good reason. Watching these bull riders attempt an eight-second ride felt like an eternity, it always left the crowd's heart racing! The wild horse race was my personal favorite. Watching seasoned cowboys try to stay on a wild horse was hilarious!

Course, the cherry on top, for me, was having my dad, better known around cowboy circles as, *"Preacher Jim,"* called up to the announcer's stand to say the *"Cowboy's Prayer."* There is no better picture I can paint of South Dakota than the song Trace Adkins sings. The lyric says, *"Old men still take off their hats and they hold 'em over their hearts…And it's always gonna be tha*t *way."*

We usually had the horses loaded and the days picnic supplies all cleaned up before the bull riding started because we knew the firework show would follow directly afterwards. We would all climb on top of the horse trailer and await the firework show that would light up the night sky. I am convinced God hung all the stars over the great plains; everywhere else just gets flickers of leftovers.

With the last kabooms of fireworks still echoing in the background, Mom and Dad would load sleepy girls into the truck and head for home.

It has been twenty years since those memorable Fourth of July days, but without fail, on the *"Fourth,"* my sister and I, along with my folks, will call one another and make comments like, *"Mom, you got the fried chicken ready?" "Dad, are the horses loaded for the big day?" "I bet Mr. Harvey is sitting in his usual spot downtown, ready to watch us ride by."*

There is something magical in traditions that never change. I am reminded of a quote by John Quincy Adams. He told a reporter, *"Duty is ours. Results are God's."* Although he was talking patriotically about the citizens of this blessed land, I often think of this when raising Eva. Magical traditions must be so imprinted upon her heart that she can't help but repeat them. The duty is mine; the result is God's.

Welcome Home

"Live as people who are free, not using your freedom as a cover-up for evil, but living as servants of God." 1 Peter 2:16

IN A PASTURE SOMEWHERE

CS Lewis said, *"The homemaker has the ultimate career. All other careers exist for one purpose only – and that is to support the ultimate career." My mother had the ultimate career.* She was always tending to us girls or busying herself with the cooking and cleaning. She wasn't just a wonderful homemaker. She was the home. One thing she has often told me was, *"I may have been the heart of our home, but your Daddy was the glue."* "He kept us all together."

I read an article in a magazine, years ago titled, *"In a Pasture Somewhere."* As I read through the article, I saw my childhood memories flash before me…

I grew up watching my dad throw a leg over the saddle every morning and lead his horse to water every night. I can still hear the sound of his boots and spurs as they would hit the boot jack when he would come in after a long day of riding in a pasture somewhere.

Dad had ways about him that are only learned in the country. For example, driving down the open highway, he spots a five-gallon bucket laying off in the ditch. He quickly hit the brakes and moved to the shoulder of the road as if he had spotted gold. He jumped out, grabbed the bucket and tossed it into the back of the truck, saying, *"You can't have too many of these around the barn!"* Better still, I have seen my dad stop on a gravel road, get out and walk right up to a rattlesnake. He proceeded to grab it by the tail, swing it around in the air and slam it to the ground while my sister and I looked on through the windshield in utter amazement. It was jaw-dropping.

I have personally been on the phone with my father as he lined up lunch with his shotgun. Come to find out he was standing on his back porch. He joked by saying, *"I like my lunch fresh and hot."* Oh, but my favorite is the one my mom tells about dad grabbing an opossum when it tried to invade the chicken coop. She said he grabbed it by the tail, threw it in the air, and had target practice on its way down. If there is one thing he has taught his girls it was, *"A country boy can survive."*

Oh, but more than all his funnies, I love my dad's gentle ways. Like the way he loved my mother or always took time with his girls.

We would be on our way to a pasture somewhere, and I can still see his hand laid over the steering wheel as we would fly down the gravel road. It was customary to raise your hand slightly and give a two-fingered wrist wave when you passed another vehicle. Although country people do not understand the meaning of the word traffic, they wrote the definition to the word neighbor.

That particular day, we were headed to load round hay bales. I was eager to go because I knew it meant I was going to get to drive the truck and flatbed trailer while he loaded the bales with the tractor.

When Dad had ranch work that required a helpful hand, he would alternate between my sister and me. Sometimes it would be exciting work like driving the truck for him; other times, it was less exciting and involved more work like stacking square bales. Now, typically, if it was square bales, the whole family would go, which meant a long day of loading bales onto a flatbed trailer and then unloading them into the barn. Still, there was a ham sandwich, coke, and snickers bar to look forward to on the lunch break!

However, for this job, I was enough; one driver for the truck and one driver for the tractor. I felt all grown up, helping dad out there in a pasture somewhere. Unbeknownst to me, he was loading more than just hay bales. He was capitalizing on moments to teach me about life and love. I saw his patience in action when I would make a mistake, but most of all, I knew how proud he was of me when he would rest his arm over my shoulder and tell me what a great job I had done.

My father made sure his girls understood that hard work was a family past-time; personal responsibility was ours alone. In a pasture somewhere, there was a work ethic being cultivated; only time would reveal it.

I can remember one summer, a neighbor told us we could go and pick all the corn we wanted from his cornfield. Mom and Dad took him literally and had us out there, filling the entire truck bed with corn. The back of the truck looked like the Corn Palace when we were finished. Except, that was only the beginning. The next day was a complete assembly line of shucking, creaming, and freezing the mountain of corn they thought we needed in our freezer. We had creamed corn, whole kernel corn, and corn on the cob. My mother looked like a mini version of Paul Bunyan holding that electric cutting knife to shave off those ears of corn. She would look up every so often and yell out the back door for more corn! It brings a lot of laughs around their table today.

Watching those cultivating years sprout, I can see that it was never about baling hay or shucking corn. It wasn't even about riding fences or branding cattle. Cutting firewood together kept the winters warm, but it wasn't about that either. Dad was leaving his mark on all of us.

His old cowboy hat still carries the marks of the dust, dirt and grime from those long hard rides. The sweat from honest money earned is forever stained inside the rim of that old hat as a constant reminder of the life he carved out for his family – in a pasture somewhere.

Welcome Home

"And let us not grow weary in doing good, for in due season we will reap if we do not lose heart." Galatians 6:9

All for a Cinnamon Roll

The ocean view was breathtaking. I could hear the waves crashing on the shore and smell the salty ocean air as I sat on the balcony of our favorite vacation spot. The dolphins were putting on quite a show that morning. Eva was two-years-old and simply squealed with excitement as she watched them jump up in the air and come crashing down into the water!

I decided it was a perfect morning for a delicious cinnamon roll from the bakery just up the road. They were homemade and were always warm and gooey. The frosting was an inch thick and would run down the sides like melting snow.

It was a quiet area where we were vacationing, so bike riding was the mode of transportation I chose. I strapped Eva into the attached wagon and made sure I had put the money in my pocket. I then jumped on the bike, and we headed out for our tasty treasure. We peddled up the steep hill and pulled into the quaint shopping square where the bakery sat overlooking the ocean. When I turned the corner, there was a semi-truck in the middle of the parking lot, so I had to maneuver around it in order to get up to the bakery. I saw the gentlemen unloading bicycles and greeted him with a cheerful *"Good Morning"* as we passed by. I parked the bike in front of the bakery and jumped off. The kickstand on the bike was a little short, so the bike toppled over when I reached down to unbuckle Eva from the wagon. I stood it back up and continued to get Eva out.

We walked up to the door and noticed the sign read, *"Closed until 9 am."* It was only eight-thirty so I decided we would just wait at the condo. I strapped Eva in again and peddled back around the man unloading bicycles. I gave a brief nod as we passed. Then, we went flying down the hill laughing the whole way down!

After thirty minutes had passed, I buckled Eva and began the intense climb, peddling back up the hill. Of course, I had to go by the gentlemen unloading bicycles, yet again. So, I smiled slightly as we passed by.

I parked the bike and forgot about the kickstand. The bike toppled over again. I sat it back up and continued to get Eva unbuckled. Eva was so excited to go into the bakery. She could smell the delicious cinnamon and nutmeg that filled the air. I said good morning to the lady behind the counter and told her we would like three of her finest cinnamon rolls!

As she was preparing our order, I reached in my pocket for the money and came up empty. Panic set in! My mind was racing as to where I could have put the money. Where could the money have gone? I sheepishly told the lady I had misplaced my money but would be back for our order.

I grabbed Eva by the hand, and we walked outside. I sat my sunglasses on the porch railing to check my pockets and pat my clothing one more time; nothing. I breathed a heavy sigh while I strapped Eva back in the wagon and got back on the bike myself. I peddled around the bicycle man and was just about to head down the big hill when I spotted the money lying on the ground! I reached down and picked it up. I made a U-turn and headed back to the bakery!

When we walked in, I shouted, *"I found it!"* The lady laughed as we exchanged money for cinnamon rolls. We left, and I put the cinnamon rolls into the front basket of the bicycle. During my buckling in of Eva, I moved the wagon slightly, which caused the bike to, you guessed it, topple over. Cinnamon rolls and money went everywhere!

Still contained in the box, I looked at the mess on the ground and just began to laugh! Eva joined me, whole-heartedly.

I did, however, want to bury my head because now the bicycle man had stopped unloading and was just staring at me. I needed a sticker across my back that said, *"I used to be cool."*

With the wind and sea breeze whisking past me as Eva and I flew down the hill, I realized I had left my sunglasses on the porch of the bakery.

I just shook my head and turned the caravan BACK around AGAIN. I was wishing for my hat as I peddled back by the bicycle gentlemen. I searched and searched but came up empty. Flying down the hill without my sunglasses, a thought occurred to me, *"The bicycle man stole my sunglasses!"*

Chuck is a no-nonsense kind of guy, and I am more like *Amelia Bedelia.* Nonsense just kind of finds me. So, he just looked at me, speechless, while I told him what transpired over the last hour. Before I could finish my theory on the lost sunglasses, Chuck was out the door, headed straight to the bicycle shop next door to the bakery.

When he arrived, he told the owner he had reason to believe the delivery man out front had stolen his wife's sunglasses. As he leaves the shop empty-handed, the owner from the bakery, next-door walked up to him and said, *"I over-heard your conversation, and I believe these are your wife's sunglasses."* "She left them on the porch railing earlier when she was looking for her money." Chuck smiled and thanked the man. As he pulled out to leave, he too, had to go around the bicycle man, who was still unloading bicycles. I imagine he had quite a story to share that night.

As for me, I sat down to a lopsided cinnamon roll with frosting no longer visible and dared anyone to come near me. I enjoyed every single bite!

Welcome Home

"Laughter does good like a medicine..." Proverbs 17:22

Mother's Biscuits

It may seem somewhat strange, but I enjoy walking through old cemeteries and reading the headstones. I love to find the oldest grave and imagine what was going on at that time or what it may have looked like around the area.

I was doing just this with a good friend of mine awhile back. We were admiring a beautiful old church and passed by its' cemetery in the courtyard. I read an epitaph from the 1800's, it stated, *"Gifted with a brilliant mind yet she confined her mental gifts to the making of a home with wonderful tact and talent. She was a Christian woman."*

To me, no finer words could be spoken over a wife and a mother. She knew where she was needed most, and although she apparently was gifted at many things, she guarded her time and made sure her family came first. Stability for her family was more important than her talents.

My mother confined many of her talents in the same manner. She taught me the value of keeping things constant, like familiar things, I could always count on. Although simplistic in nature, their value to me is incomparable. Sweet tea was always in the refrigerator, pecan pie was served at Thanksgiving, cornbread went with her vegetable soup, and mother's biscuits are still something to write about.

I can see her making these biscuits as if I were right there with her. Flour covers everything, including her. The recipe is so old it's more like a suggestion than a recipe. When she taught me to make them, it was *"A handful of this and a pinch of that."*

She prepares her dough then sprinkles flour on the counter so she can pat it out by hand. Then she cuts out perfect circles with her forty-year-old tomato paste can, better known as *"Mom's Biscuit Cutter."* Pampered chef hasn't made an equal. After she cuts out her biscuits, she lays them in her iron skillet, flipping them on both sides, so they are nicely coated with oil (*this is not a subscription to nutrition monthly*). She then slides them into the oven, where the magic takes place.

Homemade biscuits were always served on Sundays with roast and potatoes and occasionally on Saturday mornings with a big breakfast. The biscuits weren't too big, so we could always have two without feeling guilty! A light crunch followed the first bite while a soft and warm inside finished it off. Butter and homemade jelly made a perfect match for the light and flaky biscuit.

I don't know if her biscuits would win any awards anywhere other than at her own kitchen table, but they are enjoyed by all our family and friends.

Chuck and I knew there was going to be a lot of uncertainty tangled up in absolutes during our transition process. We knew we were going to have to forge ahead even with a lot of unanswered questions. Faith will require trust when many of the answers you're seeking are still unknown. It is only in the soil of uncertainty that faith is truly tested.

In the midst of an empty house and with all our life's precious memories packed away in boxes, I felt as if our family was losing sight of who we were. The process was taking longer than expected, fifteen months. Seeing the excitement on the new owners' faces only disheartened us more because we had no clear direction or destination. They had closure. We, on the other hand, were just beginning.

We moved from our lovely home to a thirty-one-foot camper that possessed one problem after the next. As time marched on, we had to make yet another move, an in-law suite apartment, while we continued to await the final word for our new destination.

At three-years-old, Eva's entire world was changing drastically. She found Mommy and Daddy as the only constant in her little life. She was such a trooper through the entire saga. Even so, I began to notice everywhere we went, she would cling to me and didn't want me out of her sight. Places she once loved, she no longer wanted to be without Daddy or me. I started connecting the dots and quickly realized I needed to create an atmosphere that reminded her of home. I needed *"Mother's Biscuits."*

I can look back and see the comfort and security simple constants produced in my life. Not that biscuits have created stability for me but what they symbolize has. I now needed to do the same for Eva.

I set to work immediately by taking pictures I had on our refrigerator at our first house and put them on the camper refrigerator. I also took her artwork and hung it up all over the wall. I found a few picture frames in storage and placed them around as well. We also set TV trays up as our kitchen table, and we all sat lined up on the couch together, with a few sarcastic jokes thrown in about the current situation.

We began to leave a trail that marked familiar in Eva's life. Safety is found in the simplicity of constancy.

Every child needs a true North. Without it, you cannot determine the other cardinal compass points.

It is said that the pioneers, who headed out west in the wagon trains, pointed their wagons toward the North Star at night, so in case, when they woke in the morning, and it was cloudy, they knew which way was west, even in a sea of grass.

Leave a compass for your children, a true North, so when they wake up on cloudy mornings, they will know which way is home.

Welcome Home

"And you will hear a voice behind you saying, this is the way, walk in it." Isaiah 30:21

Because I Said So

It is easy to spot a mother of a toddler; she is the one with smoke coming out of her ears.

As funny as that sounds, some days honestly feel that way. Most mornings, in my quiet time, I start off by jokingly telling the Lord to just hit the high points on where I blew it as a mother the day before.

At Eva's first pediatric appointment, her doctor looked at Chuck and I and said, *"Have you both read the latest book on parenting?"* Chuck and I looked at each other and said, *"No?"* To this, she replied, *"Good, Eva hasn't read it either."* We chuckled at the truth of her statement.

Children do not come with an instruction manual. I wish I could turn to page 237 of the *"EVA JEWEL MANUAL"* and have *"step by step"* directions laid out for me as to how I am suppose to handle things like socks between her toes, snagged pieces of hair caught in her hairbows, or irritating crinkles in the seat belt when it is latched. So many finicky things that are unique to each child makes a mother wonder how to handle each one?

There are days that are an endless stream of questions filled with *why*. I kind of feel like Andy Griffith when he looked down at Opie and said, *"And to think I was happy when you learned to talk."*

I remember one day, I was correcting Eva over something she could not understand. She was whining, and I had my angry face on, as she likes to call it. As I was trying to explain to her something beyond her years of understanding, I paused and recalled something Chuck often says to me, *"We do not negotiate with toddlers."*

At that moment, I looked down and said, *"Eva Jewel, the reason is simple…BECAUSE I SAID SO."* I told her the matter was closed, and if the whining continued, a firm hand would be applied to the seat of knowledge. It took a few minutes, but she knew I would follow through with my word.

Later that day, Eva asked me if I still had my angry face on? I laughed and told her no. I explained that mommies don't keep angry faces on for very long, but sometimes it takes crinkled eyebrows and a long pointer finger to teach hard lessons.

Parenting is not for the faint of heart. It can feel like a

constant battle of second-guessing yourself, but when obedience follows where disobedience once was, glimmers of hope shine through.

As a child, I was not thankful at all for my parent's discipline, but today it leads me when correcting Eva.

Proverbs 29:17 says, *"Discipline your children and they will give you peace, they will bring you delights you desire."* I have found this to be so true. Correct discipline done privately will show up publicly.

In 1 Chronicles 13:11, there is an interesting story that takes place. To paraphrase, David has gone to bring back the Ark of the Covenant to Jerusalem. In transporting the ark, they had a brilliant idea. They would place the ark on a cart. After all, it made more sense to do it this way. With all their modern conveniences, this was more practical than the way God had commanded it to be carried, which was upon the Priest's shoulders. The oxen that were pulling the cart stumbled. So, a man named Uzza reached out his hand to steady the ark. God struck him dead instantly. David became angry with God; it didn't matter that his own intellectual decisions got Uzza killed. The blame had to be pinned somewhere, and God fit the bill.

Had David transported the Ark of the Covenant the way God commanded, he would have avoided the whole incident. God, however, is unmoved. He doesn't even acknowledge David's outburst, nor does he explain to him his reasons why.

How many times have I taken matters into my own hands instead of handling correction the way God intended me to do?

Love operates within the confines of boundaries. There will be times the only answer I can give will be the same one God outlined here in this story. Hidden between the lines are the words so plainly seen… BECAUSE I SAID SO.

Welcome Home

"Children obey your parents in the Lord, for this is right"

Ephesians 6:1.

More Days Like Today

There are some days spent with family that go down in the memory book as simply delightful.

We had a day like this not too long ago. It was a day packed full of smiles and laughter as we swung on the park swings and remembered what it was like to ride on the merry-go-round as kids. Eva convinced us that ice-cream with sprinkles would be a perfect ending to our mid-morning outing.

The afternoon continued to move slowly as we hand washed the car and played in the suds bucket. We rounded out the day with a big splash as we all jumped in the pool to cool off from the summer sun. That night, after the sun had already set behind the hills, Chuck told me, *"I want more days just like today."* I smiled as I closed my eyes for a peaceful night's rest. I couldn't have agreed more.

The start to a new week came without warning. Chuck had to work out of town, and I was in charge of holding down the fort until he got back. Unfortunately, *Murphy's Law* moved in before Chuck could get down the driveway. By noon I found myself half a day behind according to my well-structured schedule.

Eva and I had started off our day outside. She was playing in the creek, and I was walking around getting my morning calisthenics when I noticed Maximus had disappeared down under the road. All of a sudden, I heard him sound the alarm! He was barking and growling to let me know he was on the job. I couldn't quite see what he had cornered, but I knew it was in a foul mood by the hissing and deep growling I heard. I yelled for Eva to go get on the picnic table while I checked it out.

I forgot about Samson in all the commotion but not to worry, he came bounding through the water to rescue Maximus. Samson was ready for his turn with the intruder. He grabbed hold of the animal by the scruff of the neck and gave it some intense shakes like a puppy with a new chew toy. Chuck and I have seen many mock battles between our dogs, but this time was not a drill.

I stood there with my mouth wide open as I watched the boys maul this animal. I finally got positioned where I could catch a glimpse and saw that it was a raccoon.

The scene looked like a chaotic boxing match. I was now in

the ring with Samson and Maximus along with their opponent Mr. Racoon. I kept sounding the bell for time, but no one was listening. Behind me, Eva was still standing on top of the picnic table, shouting, *"Get those fellas, Mommy!"* The raccoon finally managed to get the edge on Maximus. He got in a couple of good licks before he ran off.

It obviously goes without saying, the mischief these boys find themselves in keeps us on our toes and keeps their shot records current.

By the time the ruckus was calmed, and we saw the aftermath, Eva and I decided we might need to bathe down the boys. They were battle-worn and smelly. It seemed, during our dog washing escapade, more water found us than it did the fellas. We were soaked clean through.

I looked over my shoulder at my neatly arranged schedule and felt like Cinderella when she says, *"Oh, well, I guess my dress will just have to wait."*

What a disaster the day had been. The mountain of laundry never moved, my projects were never glanced at, and I ended up burning supper to the point of no return. And yet, out of the corner of my eye, I caught Eva flying through the house in her Princess Elsa play dress like nothing out of the ordinary happened at all that day. I found gratitude quickly filled the space where frustration had been.

I drifted off to sleep that night to the sound of the boys doing laps around the house. I am sure they were hot on the trail of another intruder that threatened to breach the perimeter.

In my slightly coherent state, I decided not to investigate. After all, in all of life's mishaps and unfinished intentions, I wouldn't mind more days just like today…

Welcome Home

"Let the morning bring me word of your unfailing love. For I have put my trust in You. Show me the way I should go, For to you I entrust my life." Psalms 143:8

Oh Be Careful Little Eyes What You See

When my sister and I were little, my parents guarded carefully what we were exposed to. I can remember being led out of the movie theater when they found the advertised *"Family Movie"* to be anything but family-oriented.

Many times, they would shut the TV off in the house if something did not meet their standard of what our little eyes should be seeing.

On more than one occasion, I have witnessed my father speak up in public settings if the conversation was unbecoming for young ears. His family was always his first responsibility, and he did not take his position lightly.

I can remember one occasion quite well. We were traveling South to see our Grandparents, and we stopped at a restaurant to eat. There was a man sitting in the booth behind us talking on his cell phone (this was a new phenomenon in those days). The man was talking so loudly, yelling and cursing to whoever was on the other end.

My father turned around and politely asked the man to please take his conversation elsewhere since his family was within earshot of all his obscenities.

The man very aggressively stood up and left. A few moments later, an older man and his wife, who had been sitting across the restaurant and witnessed the encounter, got up and walked over to my father. The old man told him how much he appreciated him speaking up. He told my father that was a rare find anymore.

I can't help but wonder how Chuck and I would have responded if it had been us sitting there that day?

A good friend of ours gave us some great advice once. He and his wife have two children, a few years older than Eva. He told us that there would be times when it is unpopular, even hard to speak up, but no one will protect your children like you will. He is a Marine. So, you can imagine his stance when it comes to his little girls.

We found this advice useful when a new release showed up at the box office. People were flocking to it in droves. Chuck and I did a little research and found there were many things in the movie that we were not going to allow Eva to see. I remember sharing my concerns with an acquaintance of mine, who also had a small child. Their response was simply, *"Maybe she won't notice."*

There is an interesting fact about a mustard seed. It is the only seed that will not cross-pollinate. We are growing something on the inside of our children, and it is up to us what is allowed to take root. Wrong seeds planted in the garden of a child's mind will eventually sprout at the right moment giving birth to undesirable fruit. Speaking from experience, it is easier to keep undesirable fruit out than to get it out later.

We will not be able to control what our children do when they are all grown up, but while they live at home, we have the opportunity to plant healthy seeds into rich soil and trust the Lord to grow them strong.

Too much of today's entertainment very subtly drops wrong ideologies and lifestyles into the innocent playing field of a child's mind. It is our job as parents to stand guard. We are the gatekeepers.

It amazes me that at four years old, Eva already will shield her eyes at anything we have taught her is *"Not Nice."* A child will recognize a counterfeit when they have been taught what the original looks like.

Standing in a local store a couple of years ago, I heard a man shouting provocative language and yelling at his two-year-old son as he ran around uncontrollably. It was so intense that many people found it extremely uncomfortable. I noticed they were quickly gathering their items to checkout. I looked down and saw big tears in Eva's eyes. She fearfully reached for the protective arms of her Mommy.

My Father's response in that restaurant, from all those years ago, came rushing back to me. I dropped everything in my shopping basket and headed for the exit. Eva's eyes were looking to me for guidance. She was trusting me to protect her.

The words of that old song hang framed on the wall of Eva's room as a silent reminder, no matter the innocence of the moment, I must be on guard; ever watchful as to what is allowed to penetrate into the forefront of her mind.

"Oh, be careful little eyes what you see. Oh, be careful little eyes what you see. For the Father up above is looking down in love. Oh, be careful little eyes what you see…"

Welcome Home

"Curds and honey, he shall eat that he may know how to refuse the evil and choose the good." Isaiah 7:15

KINKS IN THE ELECTRICAL CORD

Opportunity is missed by most people because it is dressed in overalls and looks like work." Thomas Edison.

I have never seen this played out better than in the backyard of our old duplex apartment. I was playing on our swing set, and my dad needed some help rolling up his electrical cords. At that time, he kept all of his sound and keyboard equipment in the backyard shed.

I was eager to help, but I made such a tangled mess trying to figure out how to roll it up correctly. My dad saw me, obviously, and he very patiently said, *"Sis, let me teach you how to roll up that cord."* He had his work cut out for him as he untwisted and unwound all the kinks and weird loops I had put in it.

As he was standing there, rolling the cord up, from shoulder to elbow, He showed me how to unwind the loops that were going the wrong way and how to make them go the right direction.

He told me I would have to train a cord to roll up correctly. It would take a little longer, but the cord would last as long as I needed it to. On the other hand, if I didn't learn how to roll it upright, it would just become a jumbled mess, and over time, it would short out when plugged in, then new ones would have to be purchased.

I see this lesson play out all the time in life. Taking short cuts or ignoring responsibility in our own personal lives will cause kinks to develop in the cords of life. Shortcuts are the nearest cousin to laziness. At first, it doesn't matter much. After all, the cord still produces power, but eventually, a short will occur, making it more costly in the long run.

In our house, we have a few basic rules, as do most families. One of which includes hard work. Eva knows hard work produces great rewards of playtime. She knows making the bed and helping with household chores (that she can do) are a part of being in this family. It is in the seemingly mundane activities and chores of our everyday life that build success.

Joyce Meyer said, *"It is not the things that we do once that will bring the victory but the things that we do over and over again."*

There is a great *"feel good"* feeling that comes from hard work.

Nothing else will produce it. We tell Eva, as Andy Griffith said to Opie, *"Shoot for the good feeling."*

The other day a big storm came through our area, and several branches had fallen down on our property. I decided it was a job I could handle easily and would alleviate Chuck from having to do it when he got home from work. So, I put on my boots and gloves and headed across the creek to start clearing. I looked behind me, and Eva was trailing me with her boots on and gloves in hand. I had not even required it this time. She had been riding her bike, and I was going to let her enjoy it, but it made my heart swell when I heard her say, *"Mommy, we do our work first, then we can play."* She was a big help to me that day.

I love to hear my mother quote a section of a proverb that so eloquently depicts how a lazy man views today. I think of it every time a lazy thought tries to cross my mind. It goes like this...

"I went by the field of a lazy man, and by the vineyard of a man devoid of understanding; And there it was, all overgrown with thorns. Its surface was covered with nettles; its stone wall was broken down. When I saw it, I considered it well. I looked on it and received instruction: A little sleep, a little slumber, a little folding of the hands to rest; So shall your poverty come like a prowler and your need like an armed man." Proverbs 24:30-34

The lesson in the electrical cord is simple. We can go as far in life as we allow discipline to keep us.

Welcome Home

Kristen Howard

"Whatever your hands find to do, do it with all of your might."
Ecclesiastes 9:10

Bosom Friends

Anne Shirley, from *"Anne of Green Gables,"* desired a bosom friend, as she called it. Someone who shared the same interests and attitudes similar to her own. She had been an orphan and had never known the meaning of true friendship. That is until she met Diana Berry, who became her very best friend for life.

I cannot think of anything more refreshing than a friend that can read your thoughts before you say them. Someone who knows your winks, stares, sideways glances, and throat clears; someone who you can call and even though utter chaos is on the other end of the phone line, you are able to say, *"I know now isn't a good time, but I just have to unload."*

My sister and I could not fit this description more. We are as different as night and day, but instead of trampling upon each other's differences, we have learned to give each other room and embrace those things we have in common, which are many.

Growing up, I was *"Miss Prissy,"* and Brittney was a *"Tomboy."* If my shoes got a little muddy, I cried. Yet, Brittney would be in the backyard, making herself into a full-bodied human mud pie! I was always easy for Mother to clean up, but my sister, on the other hand, required lots of elbow grease! She wasn't afraid of anything and was a perfect tag along for my dad during his horse breaking years.

No matter how different we were as kids when the lights went out, we would crawl into each other's bed and drift off to sleep, giggling.

We are still giggling together as grown-ups, yet we live very differently. I live my life by a detailed plan and a fully loaded, timed schedule. In picture form, I'm in a kayak racing down the river, dodging sharp rocks, rapids, and waterfalls. My sister, no matter the occasion, just an ordinary day or hosting a party for forty-five, manages an uninterrupted leisure float down a lazy river, with an iced-lemonade in hand. NOTHING ruffles her feathers.

Brittney is one of the funniest people you will ever be around. It is nothing that she tries to do, it never draws a crowd, and it is only enjoyed by those who know her best.

I remember one day, a few years back, I got trapped in an

extremely awkward conversation with a stranger explaining to me how they *"Bird Fed"* each one of their children when they were babies. My eyes were like saucers, and I stared dumbfounded at how my courteous *"Hello"* could have gotten me into this awkward conversation. I figured it was because I was holding my infant at the time. Unbeknownst to me, my sister was within earshot of this conversation. Instead of walking in to save me, she sends me a text message. It read, *"I'm crying, laughing right now."* I knew she had decided it was more entertaining to watch me weasel out of this conversation than for her to run to my rescue! We have shared many laughs over that strange encounter.

My sister is the type of person that prefers to do things behind the scenes to help people. She is the type of friend that will do that which is least expected to be a blessing in someone's life.

During the first few weeks after we brought Eva home from the hospital, it was extremely trying. Chuck had gone back to work, and I was left at home, staring at a screaming baby who loved to be held. It did not matter what was going on or what needed to be done. As long as I held her, she was, for the most part, perfectly fine.

Every time she would drift off to sleep in my arms, I would sit down with her and let out a sigh of relief, only to realize my book or the remote was just out of reach. So, there I would be, stuck staring out the window, too afraid to move.

There is a learning curve with a new baby. It's like sandpaper pressing against our selfishness. Little ones will create in us the ability to be our best selves by stripping off the worst of us.

One such *"Sandpaper"* day, I was beyond frustrated. Out of the blue, my sister called. She and her husband have a little boy just one year older than Eva, Benjamin James. So, she could pretty much guess what my pressure gauge was reading.

I was in the middle of changing Eva's diaper for what seemed like the fiftieth time that day, and well…I was just mad; covered in spit up, burp cloths draped over my shoulder, and unable to finish anything I started, left me feeling helpless.

Shortly after hanging up the phone with her, I heard the doorbell ring. When I opened the door, there my sister stood with her arms stretched out.

All she said was, *"Give her to me."* With tears in my eyes, Brittney took Eva from me. She stripped her down to her diaper, wrapped a cool blanket loosely around her, and sat down with her. Eva was asleep in seconds.

Then she looked at me and told me to go do whatever I needed to do. I went and cleaned the garage (completely normal for me). After I finally completed something that would last longer than thirty minutes, I took a hot shower.

Honestly, there was no real physical rest for me that day or the days to follow. Eva was still going to need me in a few hours, but the peace that flooded my mind changed my outlook. I was able to catch my breath and find the strength I needed to press on. God's strength is made perfect in weakness.

I will never forget my sister's kindness to me that day—a simple act of selflessness that gave me reassurance.

Even though God could rain down blessings from heaven upon us, He doesn't. He sees the value of using people. He sees the value of bosom friends.

I kind of feel like Winnie the Pooh when he wrote about his dear friend Piglet, *"It seems they always had been and always would be friends. Time could change much, but not that."*

Welcome Home

"A friend loves at all times...." Proverbs 17:17

Remember Who You Are

It really didn't matter what we were leaving the house for; our parents never let Brittney or me leave without saying, *"Remember who you are,"* especially if we were going to spend the night at one of our friend's house.

The integrity behind it did not sink in initially, but my parents were diligent in reminding us of the importance of those words.

First and foremost, we were Christians and needed to behave in such a way that honored Christ in everything we said and did. Secondly, we carried our family name everywhere we went. Brittney and I became a direct reflection of our upbringing in the absence of our parents. Of course, we were far from perfect and made many mistakes, but Mom and Dad were always there to see that mistakes were mended and dealt with accordingly.

In their own way, Mom and Dad would talk to us about the importance of character.

Dad would tell us to be a trustworthy friend. He would tell us not to pick fights but be a peacemaker, and then he would whisper, *"But if you have to fight, make sure you win!"*

Mom would tell us to be a blessing while at our friend's house and to pick up after ourselves. We were not to be a hindrance to the plans that others had laid out. We were to always remember we were a guest in someone else's home.

These things seem so simple, but it is easy to look around and see so many of these principles are not being taught anymore.

I had a lady tell me that school is where children learn the mechanics for life; that is where they find their fit and where they gain an understanding of who they are. My mind was racing with responses that went something like, *"Now I can rest easy. I am so glad we have given up our rights as parents and handed it to the schools. The evidence is overwhelming as to what a great job they are doing."* I verbalized the parts that seemed to fit.

Teachers are a gift from God, and I am so very thankful for the teachers in our schools that teach right thinking into the minds of our children. I had many teachers like this growing up. I consider them jewels in my life and would not trade any of my precious school days. They were valuable and taught me so much.

At the same token, it is not the school's job to teach our

children who they are. That starts in the home. It is our job as parents to make sure we are placing in our children the right morals and values that line up with God's Word. That is the only truth that leaves their feet on a firm foundation. All else will be sinking sand.

When Eva was about a year and a half, she would try to bite her little friends. Of course, all children do this. They are learning boundaries and how to defend their own territory. When her teacher approached me about the problem, I was embarrassed that my perfect child would do something like this! I quickly told her teacher that Chuck and I would handle this.

She gently put her hand on my arm and, in conversation, said, *"Taking Eva home and correcting something that she doesn't even remember doing will not fix the problem. You will have to be intentional and correct her in the act. Then pray for her so she can hear you. The God inside of her is not small. He knows how to lead her."* What a concept to this Christian mother who did not even think of that!

I began to take time showing Eva how to share. It is hard when there are no other siblings in the house, so I used opportunities where I was involved. Then, on the way to her preschool each morning, I would pray out loud that the Lord would help her to be kind and learn to share with her friends.

Would you believe it worked?! Not that we never had another incident of her not sharing, but the biting stopped, and her ability to share only improved.

Eva is a direct reflection of her father and me everywhere she goes. Even at four years old, people are catching a glimpse into our home through the actions of our child.

Fredrick Douglass said, *"It is easier to build strong children than it is to repair broken men."*

What we speak over our children is so powerful. Proverbs 18:21 says, *"Life and death are in the power of the tongue and those that love it will eat its fruit."*

I wrote this prayer that I pray over Eva, and I am believing to see good fruit from it as she grows...

"Father, I pray that you would help Chuck and I be the kind of parents that Eva can be proud of. Help us to teach her who she is in You. Her worth is not found in people, places or things, but in Christ alone. Help me, as Mommy, to be graceful under pressure. I pray you would help Eva as she goes through this day to be kind and caring that she would share with her friends and be helpful where she is needed. Lord, she may be young, but You are not. I pray she would hear Your voice and never follow another; teach her to fear You. Give her Godly friends and a teachable spirit; Surround her with Your favor. Give Your angels charge over her and keep your hand of protection upon her as she lives out her life fully pleasing You in the talents You have placed upon her. And Lord, above all, let her remember who she is to You. – Amen."

Welcome Home

Kristen Howard

"I praise you for I am fearfully and wonderfully made." Psalms 139:14

HAPPY CAMPER

Camping was always a big adventure for our family. Sometimes we would do big camping trips, like going out to the Black Hills of South Dakota. Other times we would do small camping trips in town at a local campground. Either way, we knew sleeping bags, picnic tables, campfires, and smores would be included. Among other activities, swimming, hiking and fishing completed a camping trip.

I remember one camping trip that took us to Nebraska, where we tubed down a very well-known river called the Niobrara River. That night a very intense thunderstorm forced us out of our tent. Mom and I ended up in the cab of the truck while Dad and Brittney moved the air mattress underneath a picnic pavilion and roughed it. They were always more daring than Mom and me. Of course, the morning sun came and dried out all the campsites.

Another time, our family vacation took us to Washington state to visit family. The folks thought it would be a great idea to put a red topper over the bed of Dad's silver truck and camp each night on our trek out west. The topper made a nice bed for Mom and Dad to sleep in, while Brit and I got the cab of the truck; a little less cozy I can assure you. We could hear dad snoring through the windows while the seatbelts were digging into our sides.

Each morning when we woke, Dad would start the day off by saying, *"The key word for this vacation is FLEXIBLE."* Brittney and I would just look at each other, concluding that the only people *"FLEXIBLE"* on this trip, was us.

Thinking of all these funny camping stories made me want to create my own with my family. So, we decided to arrange a camping trip with some friends of ours.

I had everything neatly arranged and ready for packing when Chuck got home from work. He got us all loaded, and off we went! Our family arrived first, and we staked claim to two tent camping sites.

The first thing we did was get rid of some pesky red ants that had invaded the area by starting a campfire. Next, we began to set up our picnic tent. I made the mistake of purchasing a screened

Home Sweet Home

tent that had to be put together piece by piece (a mistake that would correct itself in the future). Every time we had the poles on one side put together and positioned, the poles on the other side would fall out.

Frustration was creeping in quickly. I caught the eyes of Chuck a couple of times and realized I should probably just quit talking.

Once we finally got the picnic tent standing, chuck began to stake the lines down. He turned around to grab his mallet when a breeze swept through the campground. The tent took flight before we could grab it. It looked like a new kind of hot air balloon. As quickly as it went up, it gracefully came down and landed in our campfire! We started running to get the tent out of the fire before it all went up in flames! We could feel our hearts beating through our sweaty clothes as we pulled a half-seared tent out of the fire. Dusting off the ashes, we could see that only one side was burned. We scathed by thankfully, managing to save the tent.

By this point, we were ready to pack up and go home, but we chose to press on. We laid out our sleeping tent, and each had a side ready to raise when *"Campers of America"* pulled in beside us. These people had a brand-new hybrid camper. The man effortlessly backed in his new camper, got out and used a heavy-duty extension cord to plug his camper into the electrical outlet. We watched him push a button, and both ends of his camper folded out into instant comfortable beds.

Chuck and I, still standing there holding our tent stakes, watched this man casually extend his awning and set up lounge chairs. From the storage beneath, he proceeded to pull out a brand new flat top George Foreman grill.

At that moment, he looked over at us and must have recognized our look because he just smiled and said, *"I did the tent camping last year with my family. After that experience, with my wife and two toddlers, I left and went straight to purchase this new camper."*

I looked over at Chuck and said, *"Do you want me to start loading the truck now or wait five?"* We both just started laughing and decided to continue putting up the tent.

That night as we slept on a leaking air mattress, we dreamed of those comfy beds at the campsite next door, but the sharp rocks gouging into our backs snapped us to reality.

Before we ever left for our first camping adventure, a friend of mine told me, *"There are going to be mishaps and mistakes but make the most of it, laugh a lot. If you do, camping will be the best memories you ever make."*

Her advice held true. As nice as the campsite was next to us, I wouldn't have traded our experience for one night in that cozy bed.

Since that summer, we have camped many times, and yet none have even come close to that experience.

Dissatisfaction likes to creep in to rob family fun and steal the joy. It is only when we can find the humor in the *"FLEXIBILITY"* that will ultimately make us a *"Happy Camper."*

Welcome Home

"Better is a dry morsel with quiet than a house full of feasting with strife." Proverbs 17:1

Cheese and Crackers

He threw the truck in reverse and slammed on the gas. We sped out of the driveway. My sister and I were crying. Thoughts were racing through our little heads. Why was Mommy not in the truck? Why were they fighting? Did they not love each other anymore? Couldn't they just say *"I'm Sorry"* and fix it?

All of a sudden, he slammed on the brakes and sat there in the middle of our street for just a minute before pulling back in the driveway. He got out without saying a word and went back inside.

It was only a few hours earlier when it all began…

Mom and Dad were upstairs in our little duplex apartment on Grant Street. They were having an intense discussion about something way over a six- and seven-year old's head. There were no shouting or angry words used, but it was obvious, even to our little eyes, that something was very wrong.

Unbeknownst to us children, it was simply the growing pains of marriage. Most of the things we fight with our spouse about are not heaven or hell issues, but the effects arguing can have on children can last a lifetime.

We were right at the age where a child's mind starts to log moments away permanently. Pictures of my mother crying and my father sitting on the bed talking to her so calmly are etched in my memory banks forever.

I grabbed Brittney's little hand and pulled her downstairs. I knew what we needed to do. They needed a snack. Mommy always made us snacks when we were crying. Cheese and crackers would dry her tears and make everything better. We put the cheese and crackers together, placed them in some aluminum foil, and took them up to their bedroom. We walked out, knowing that had solved the problem.

Time went by that afternoon, and we found ourselves sitting in the front seat of Dad's pickup truck. Dad had gone inside, and we were waiting for him to come back. Our thoughts were scrambling, wondering what would happen next? Why were they still angry? Were we going to have to go see our parents at separate houses like many of my other friends? We loved them both so much. How would we ever choose? One of them was destined to be hurt.

These invasive thoughts were quietly put to rest as Brittney and I watched Dad come out the front door. He had Mother by the hand. To this day, I still do not know what he said to her when he went back inside, but I do know whatever he said hasn't changed in forty years.

Brittney and I have never seen another argument or fight between them. Now, that's not to say they have never disagreed, but it has been handled behind closed doors.

My dad made a decision that day that changed what could have been a tragic end to their love story. Cheese and crackers didn't fix the problem, choosing to *stay* did.

What my father didn't know was how his decision would rescue *me* many years later. My mother's fiery red hair must be woven somewhere in the roots of my brown hair because I too, found myself wanting my own way.

I got in my car and left the house in a huff. I made it about a mile down the road when I pulled off. I sat there and began to cry. I prayed for the Lord to help me. I was right, and I was mad. I closed my eyes and, in an instant, I saw my father's old truck pull back in the driveway. I knew I had to go home. I had fences to mend.

Later that day, Chuck asked me why I came back? He thought it was only to save face. Normally he would have been right. We all want to look good and show off our perfect lives to everyone we meet. However, that was not the case this time. Through my tears, I shared with him about *"Cheese and Crackers."* I told him I loved *us* more than I loved being right.

I heard it said once, *"Christians aren't the perfect people, they are the getting back up people."* My parents have left a legacy of *"Getting back up."* Those early lessons are still echoing in their actions each day.

On September 10th, 2020, my parents celebrated forty years of marriage. They have proven the grass is not greener on the other side. They have shown by example that the grass is greener where it is watered.

My parents are more in love today than forty years ago when they said, *"I DO."* Mom and Dad always sit close to one another and holding hands for them happens without a thought. It's as if they are telling the world, *"Happily Ever After"* does exist.

We never know how our decisions will affect others, but know this, someone is always watching.

To this day, cheese and crackers are one of my favorite snacks, and I often think of that day with fond memories.

Mom and Dad, Thank You for staying...

Welcome Home

"Be devoted to one another in love. Honor one another above yourselves." Romans 12:10

A Handful of Dandelions

I love it when a plan comes together. Whether it is packing for a trip and everything is neatly arranged for easy access to all the little emergencies or future life plans that have come to fruition. It makes no difference to me. As long as the plan is executed and finds completion, I love it.

Although, As Tani Parker put it, *"Most days I feel like a little kid that can't get their crayon to stay in the lines of the coloring maze."* It seems so simple! But most of the time, the crayon is bigger than the tiny maze printed on the page, and yet somehow, I am expected to stay inside of the lines. It resembles life with a toddler.

About the time I have things working like clockwork, I walk my child into the men's restroom. In my humiliation, I quickly turn her around and exit, only to be confronted by another woman headed to the correct door. She just laughed and said, *"Oh, it's alright, Honey, we have all done it."*

There are a thousand mistakes we make as mothers just trying to do right by our children. We are always caught in the middle of a task with someone needing our attention. Of course, this leads us to leave out important details of the new task we have now been assigned to. We take our child's temperature and forget the Tylenol. We get their breakfast and forget the milk. We pack great snacks and forget the gummies.

It seems like there is always something forgetful in the art of motherhood. Multi-tasking can be our greatest asset and our worst enemy. I can get eleven things done at once and then forget the groceries at the store. Between you and me, I have even driven off with a bank deposit tube in my hand. It took me a few seconds to realize why everyone was honking at me. Eva didn't notice a thing. She was happily eating her sucker.

It's so easy to get lost in our shortcomings and forget all the wonderful things we do right by our families.

It was a day as described above, Eva and I were out walking, just enjoying our afternoon walk together. The dogs, of course, off running through the woods (It's better sometimes that I not know where they go). All of a sudden, Eva offered me a freshly picked bouquet of beautiful yellow flowers. She had been picking them all along the way, and I just never noticed. At that moment, all of my mistakes were erased in a handful of dandelions.

Like all mothers, I too get so wrapped up in my child that there are moments I question the meaning. I get so busy cleaning birdseed out of her little pockets and collecting *Cheese-It's* from inside her dollhouse that it is easy to think perhaps I am missing out on life's great adventure or missing my chance to make my mark on the world. And yet, it was in a handful of dandelions that showed me, *"Our greatest contribution to the world may not be something we do, but someone we raise."*

If you find yourself following a trail of Band-Aid wrappers to locate your child or perhaps multi-tasking has you a little overwhelmed, recall a handful of dandelions in your own life and remember, *"Tomorrow is always fresh with no mistakes in it."* – Anne of Green Gables

Welcome Home

"…God will keep him busy with the joy of his heart."
Ecclesiastes 5:20

LIVING WATERS FELLOWSHIP

Growing up in a Pastor's home had its advantages and disadvantages, the same as any other family. On one hand, we got free movie passes to the theatre in town, but on the other hand, my parents knew over half the town, one way or another, so I could never get away with anything!

My folks believed that teaching us how to make choices was essential in life. Dad, being the Pastor, would be at the church long before the doors were opened. Mom would come along later. Our choice concerning church was simple; we could ride with Dad or we could ride with Mom.

My memories of Living Waters Fellowship are probably tainted with fondness, but even in its imperfections, I find many principles that I value today were carved inside the walls of that church building.

It was your typical full gospel church; lively music, sound preaching, and a few *"Amens"* from the congregation. People knew one another, and relationships were genuine.

My father and my mother took the time to know their members. This rarely happened in the altar of the church, but more so over a Sunday potluck or picnic in the park. It would happen over a horse ride out in the pasture or boating with friends. Sometimes it would be just a quick *"Hello"* at Wal-Mart; other times, it was to lend a helping hand where it was needed. There were new births celebrated and funerals remorsefully performed. It was in these less than spiritual moments, where my parents chose to be present in the lives of those who called them Pastor.

To hear my father talk about shepherding a flock is to hear his heart for people. His depiction comes through many years of experience. He told me once, *"A good shepherd never has rough hands."* He explained about Lanolin, which is an oil found on wool-bearing sheep. As the shepherds would touch the wool, the Lanolin healed and softened their hands. It protected their hands from abrasions.

Some might think a pastor should keep his distance from his congregation thus to avoid being hurt; not my father. He taught me, it is not in the distance that pastors find protection but in mingling with the sheep. Pastors who do not smell like sheep will create a herd mentality, not a flock. A herd is driven; A flock is led. The shepherd needs the sheep just as much, and the sheep need the shepherd.

Even as the Pastor's daughter, I was not allowed to sit on the sidelines. I had to find an avenue to serve in. My parents believed that serving others was close to God's heart and serving in the local church ran a close second.

Today, we live in a fast-paced society where slapping a gift card in someone's hand qualifies as effort, and a sympathy meal is something that comes out of a drive-thru window. We put more thought into a text message than taking time for an actual conversation with someone. Growing up, my parents assured me, I would never be able to convenience my way out of serving.

Our previous pastor, before we moved, made a statement that resonated with me. He was speaking about Abraham going up the mountain to offer Isaac as a sacrifice. He said, *"The day Abraham climbed Mt. Moriah, he was trusting God, but Isaac was trusting his daddy."* Isaac was old enough to notice there was not a lamb with them as they climbed the mountain. All he could do was trust that his daddy knew what he was doing.

Eva will be of no effect if left to her own. Chuck and I must teach her how to be a part of a flock. My little girl is watching me. She is trusting her daddy and I to show her the way.

When Eva was a baby, we began to take her to the church nursery, and then, as she grew, to kids' church, I saw the love and exhaustion on the faces of those that were serving our children each Sunday. I could hear Pastor Randy saying, *"Is the God you love the God you serve?"* I had learned through the growing pains of my youth that serving would cost me something; time, effort and money.

I made a decision at that time in my life that I would give where Eva was taking. I would teach Eva by example how to serve. I want her to recall precious memories one day, of those that poured into her as a child, and I never want her to question where her mother was.

I will be easy to locate. She will find me making her costume for the seemingly insignificant Christmas play or helping her learn songs for the Easter program. She will find me organizing the church carnival and talent show, trying to figure out where we are going to put *"Mrs. Antwanette's"* daughter who can't sing. She will find me back in the Sunday school rooms helping prepare snack time and watching me tell all of the kids to sit down and be quiet! But most of all, she will see love and exhaustion on *my* face. She will know I served.

There is an unknown hero somewhere that tirelessly gave of themselves to make a difference in each of our lives. Now, the turn is ours.

Home Sweet Home

My life was impacted in more ways than I realized through Sunday school. Our teacher would make the Bible story come alive as she placed the characters on the felt board. My friends and I would roar with laughter as we tried to keep up with the actions of the song *Father Abraham*. I thought Gerbert had come to life when he appeared over the puppet show wall to tell me how special I was to God. My heart soared when my mother smiled at the arts and crafts I had made for her with noodles and paper plates.

As we grew up, there were youth group meetings, outings and serious talks about life and love. I can still see the faces of those that chose to pour into my life and help set me on a course for success.

Church is more than just a building where we go to be encouraged and hear a pretty sermon. It is where we are corrected, challenged and changed. It is where we go to serve and make a difference in someone's life.

Living Waters Fellowship is gone now, but the effect it had lives on in the people changed by its presence. For me, I feel its presence every time I choose to serve. Pastor Randy Fuller says, "*Sons are born, but servants are made.*"

Welcome Home

"*As each one has received a gift, minister it to one another, as good stewards of the manifold grace of God.*" 1 Peter 4:10

Paint the Dragons Red

Danger lurks everywhere for toddlers. It is disguised within our homes as an over-looked pan on a hot stove or a seemingly harmless hairdryer plugged into an obscure plug-in. Danger finds itself on the other side of the dividing line as we drive our precious cargo down the road. Danger lies in our carefree extracurricular activities that appear to be stamped with nothing but innocent fun. And yet, hidden in the corners of our carefree entertainment, danger can be waiting, anywhere, at any time.

I remember a few months back, my sister had come for a visit, and we had the kids swimming in our pool. They had been swimming for quite a while, so Brittney and I called for the kids to get out of the pool, and we lined them along the fence while we began taking off life jackets and collecting towels.

My sister and I were engaged in a little harmless chit-chatting when we heard, SPLASH! A splash that just a few minutes earlier would have been an oblivious fun-loving sound in our ears. This time, however, it was as if an alarm sounded. Both of us immediately realized what had happened. I screamed, *"Ben's in the pool!"* My sister jumped in one way, and I jumped in the other. We got to him in seconds. He had jumped into the shallow end of the pool without his life jacket on.

The life jacket had given him a false sense of security while swimming, and when it was removed, he thought he could still swim. It didn't take him long, however, to realize that was not the case. He struggled for a few seconds and swallowed a mouthful of pool water before we got to him. In a sheer panic, no one bothered to notice that he could touch the bottom, not even him.

I heard a lady say once, *"Ask the Lord to paint dragons red."* I thought it was so objective and powerful that I adopted the phrase as my own. No matter the danger, whether directly or indirectly, aimed at my family, I want dragons painted red. I want the Lord to help me be one step ahead of that which could be threatening.

There were severe repercussions from Ben's actions but most importantly, he learned a valuable lesson. He was not invisible. It was in his immediate sinking into what only a few minutes prior had been a sparkling blue pool full of splashes and giggles that now was painted red with danger. The very thing he enjoyed moments before now had the capacity to threaten his life.

Thankfully, the Lord was one step ahead of us. You see, just a few hours earlier, I had told my sister I would watch the kids at the pool while she went to town. For some reason, let's just call it *"mother's intuition,"* if you will, she said no. She just didn't feel comfortable doing that. She was confident in my abilities to watch the kids, but something gave her pause.

Could it have been the Lord painting the dragon red for her that day? Had she left me, the scene may have looked different than what played out for Ben and for myself. As a parent, the Lord has given us an inward alarm that comes prewired, built-in, to sense danger.

We will never know what *"could"* have happened that day, but one thing is for certain, when we, as parents, sense an unsettling inside of us, listen.

Whether it comes in quiet whispers or bellows from heaven, I want to hear *HIS* warnings. He can see things that I cannot.

Lord, today I pray that you would paint the dragons red so we as parents can see danger lurking in secret. Arm us with boldness and the ability to think fast on our feet. Reveal to us escapes where it is needed and show us how to slay the dragon when he rears his ugly head.

Welcome Home

"The name of the Lord is a strong tower the righteous run to it and are safe!" Proverbs 18:10 (the literal translation of the word "safe" here means…lifted out of reach!)

Twenty Winks

Benjamin Franklin said, *"Early to bed, early to rise will make a man healthy, wealthy and wise."* My dad must have lived by this quote because he was up with the chickens and went to bed with the sun. He worked hard all day long. He was never one for sitting idle.

Once, when he was heading out to the pasture, he jumped a small ditch and twisted his ankle in the landing. He came into the house and took his boot off. His ankle was the size of a baseball. He had no choice at that moment but to elevate and ice it. He was supposed to rest it for several days, but I recall the next day, he forced his foot into his boot and awkwardly hobbled back out to the barn. There was work to do for him, and no high ankle sprain was going to stop him. He believed if he were going to have anything out of this life, he'd better get to it. No one was going to do it for him.

I do not care much for idle time unless it has arrived from a productive day. However, I have come to appreciate the sound of quiet when nap time approaches for Eva Jewel. Taking a few minutes for myself to read or relax has become a welcomed reprieve from the wants and needs that lay just beyond the steady breathing of a toddler sleeping.

Chuck and I were in the negotiating stages of our new house just a few months back, and I anticipated that phone call that said: *"Offer accepted."* I would wake up excited and plow through my day, teaching classes and taking care of Eva.

One day, on our way home, I had called to say hello to my dad or *"Pa,"* as Eva lovingly calls him. Eva told him all about her morning, and I told him how antsy I was over the possibilities of getting the house we now call home. All of a sudden, Dad says, *"Well sis, I am going to take me a little nap."* I couldn't believe that in all my anticipation of this big moment we had been waiting on for months, my dad was going to take a nap! Shocked, I said, *"Dad! How can you take a nap at a time like this!?"* He responded, *"Discipline."*

In the book *God is in the Small Stuff*, the authors talk a lot about discipline. Satisfaction has a balance, and balance comes from a life lived with consistencies. Most of the time, we want an abundance of possessions and immediate simplicities. Still, nothing worthwhile comes quickly and certainly not without discipline.

We find discipline affects every area of our life; the physical, mental, financial, relational and spiritual. It is so easy to get caught up looking for instant results rather than the small victories that help us win the battle. We all want money, and we want it now, but only a few put together a plan that achieves financial success. We all want the perfect marriage and friendships, but very few put in the time it takes. We all want to look fantastic, but few eat less and exercise more.

My dad is an extremely healthy, successful, *slightly older*, but handsome man (he will like that part). He has spent his life staying disciplined. I would say he has even gotten better with age. My mother has too, but this story is about his naps, so I will stay on track. My dad's hard work and no-nonsense kind of living has played an important role in his health. He knew when to stop and just take a nap.

It actually is kind of comical because no matter the place, he would stretch out and place his cowboy hat or cap over his face and take twenty winks. I have seen the man drop his horse's reigns and stretch out under a cottonwood tree or lay the seat back in the truck while waiting on my mother. It never mattered what was going on. He could be in a crowd or alone in the house, and all of a sudden, the sound of snoring would commence. He would be out in less than ten seconds and wake up in about twenty minutes with a renewed sense of duty for what awaited next.

His short snoozes never consisted of overly comfortable positions nor pure silence. It was always a position that could be easily interrupted and made for a quick reset, never a long shut-down.

My dad is a very patient man, and he should be after raising me. When a difficult decision rested upon his shoulders, he would do the oddest thing; take a nap.

He taught us girls never to make a big decision in a hurry. Let your mind have a chance to rest. It took me several years and many impulse decisions to understand the benefits of this principle, but now I recognize that a little perspective and a nap go hand in hand.

After I hung up with my dad that day, I noticed Eva had conked out in her car seat while we rode home. I figured she had the right idea. There was no sense in wringing my hands, waiting for the phone to ring. I decided to rest my eyes as well. It was hard, but I finally laid my head back against the seat and dozed off. I woke up about fifteen minutes later feeling refreshed. My head no longer had spinning wheels attached to it.

The long-awaited phone call came that same evening, and we were the proud owners of our beautiful home. On two accounts,

I had much to be excited about! One, because we now had a place to call home. Two, I had learned peace and patience mattered more than the phone call.

Welcome Home

"Jesus was inside the boat, sleeping with his head on a pillow." Mark 4:38